a day at the Beach

Devotions to help you relax, reflect, and renew

JEDD & TODD HAFER

Tyndale House Publishers, Inc.
Carol Stream, Illinois

Visit Tyndale online at www.tyndale.com.

TYNDALE and Tyndale's quill logo are registered trademarks of Tyndale House Publishers, Inc.

A Day at the Beach: Devotions to Help You Relax, Reflect, and Renew

Designed by Mark Anthony Lane II

Edited by Anisa Baker

Published in association with the literary agency of MacGregor Literary Agency.

For information about special discounts for bulk purchases, please contact Tyndale House Publishers at csresponse@tyndale.com or call 800-323-9400.

ISBN 978-1-4964-1487-8

Printed in China

23	22	21	20	19	18	17
7	6	5	4	3	2	1

How Pope Gregory Stole Our Beach Days

For most people, the new year begins on January 1, the conventional entryway to a fresh calendar year, with all its promise and possibilities.

Not that long ago, each new year was sparked by March's spring equinox. This was back in the day when humanity was willing to follow the lead of the sun, moon, and stars for guidance in marking the times and seasons.

Not for long. Restless humanity demanded its own way. Julius Caesar introduced a new calendar that changed the start of the year from March 25 to January 1, and in 1582 Pope Gregory XIII adapted Caesar's calendar so it synced with the solar year.

England and its colonies adopted this calendar (aka the Gregorian calendar) in 1752. To reset time itself and transition to the Gregorian calendar, the British Parliament grabbed eleven days from later in the year and tossed them, unused, into history's waste bin. If you had been living in one of the American colonies during that time, you would have gone to sleep on September 2 and arisen on September 14.

We want those days back. Don't you?

Nonetheless, like you, we march according to the squarish boxes of January through December. Book due dates, school years, and quarterly tax deadlines demand it. However, for us, each new year doesn't truly begin until we can put our bare feet into the welcoming sand of a favorite beach. This ritual signals, if not the true beginning of the year, the beginning of the *best part* of the year. The time when the year becomes fully alive. Rehearsals are over. It's showtime!

Our home state, Colorado, doesn't easily release its icy winter grip. Sometimes even in late May a stubborn blanket of snow will cling to a hillside or shady slab of backyard. It wasn't that long ago that a planned multifamily road trip to Huntington Beach was postponed for several days due to a snowstorm. In June. It seemed to us that the Gregorian year had completely lost its way, like a wandering child in a megamall.

If you want to live in Colorado, you must hug the twin virtues of patience and flexibility.

On the first night originally slated for our escape, we cleaned out the fireplace and coaxed a few odd slabs of wood into a bright blaze. We watched the relentless snow-fall and listened to the wind push at the windows and rattle the front door.

Soon the fire was warm enough for those of us closest

to it to kick off our shoes and swap the hot chocolate for a cooler drink. We couldn't be at the beach, but we brought some of its peace to our indoor huddle.

The next morning, you could feel the kiss of early summer in the air even though the landscape was swaddled in snow. In the distance we heard birdsong. It was tempting to jump in the car and make up for lost time. But we decided to wait, breathe, and let the shy sun slip from behind the curtain of clouds and work its melting magic. Dry roads are worth the wait.

And the beach would be just as "there" in three days as it would in two.

So many of the best things in life are willing to wait for us. Perhaps this is God's way of telling us to embrace the anticipation rather than fight it. To surf with the tide rather than swim against it. To let the journey unfold on its own schedule so it can be savored. Good advice for road trips to the beach. And for life itself.

And so we present to you this devotional, from two brothers who love God, our families, the Denver Broncos, and beaches. Yes, our home state of Colorado isn't known as beach country, but we have our lakesides, reservoirs, and sparkling rivers. You can refresh your soul and encounter your Creator even if there isn't an ocean in the picture.

By the way, you sunburn more quickly at a Colorado "beach," but at least you don't have to worry about sharks in the water.

Of course, we love to journey to a variety of beach settings—whether on a multifamily vacation to Huntington Beach or a quiet (read: kid-free) sojourn to St. Kitts or Michigan's Grand Traverse Bay. The beach is also a great spot for nurturing our creative sides—Todd did much of his work on this book during a mini writing sabbatical at Heceta Beach on the Oregon coast.

We hope you enjoy the following collection of personal accounts, intriguing beach trivia, and even a fable or two. May your reading be as refreshing as a day at the beach, offering soothing waters for your mind and sunshine for your soul.

We also pray that you will be strengthened with all his glorious power so you will have all the endurance and patience you need. May you be filled with joy.

COLOSSIANS 1:11

Jedd and Todd Hafer

Life Unplugged

ONE OF THE true joys of a day (or even a few hours) at the beach is the freedom to unplug. No phones, no pagers, no tablets or computers.

Yes, we all appreciate the speed and convenience of modern communication, but sometimes we must say, "Enough already!" to all the buzzes and beeps, dings and pings.

Fortunately, even if you're wading in the shallow waters of the Caribbean—with no electronic gadgets in sight—you can still avail yourself of the most amazing form of communication ever invented: prayer.

The blessing of prayer allows us to stay connected to God all the time, anytime, no matter what we are doing (including diving for a conch shell or working on the perfect tan). And even if the only prayer you can muster is "Ahhhhh!" or "Arrrrrgh!!!" God understands. He knows the call of our hearts, even when words are not enough . . . or simply too much—those times when we are long on verbiage but short on coherence.

Prayer is about listening as well. After you have prayed to God, quiet your heart and mind to hear what He has to say. He longs to speak to every open spirit that is enduring the rush of the morning commute . . . or enjoying peace and quiet in a secluded spot in the woods.

So pray. Speak. Yearn. Listen. Unplug from everything but the ultimate source of life. God is near.

Never stop praying.

1 THESSALONIANS 5:17

Making the Ordinary Extraordinary

YOU'VE FOLDED THAT last T-shirt, paid all of your bills, and (finally) replaced the lifeless lightbulb.

Caught up on e-mail? Check. Urgent call returned? Affirmative.

Then, instead of crossing a few more tasks off your to-do list, you smile. Breathe deeply. You feel satisfied, centered—like you've just finished final exams and summer vacation lies ahead. Being faithful in even the small things? Such devotion elicits a reward . . . a hard-earned break. Somewhere, there is a beach with your name on it.

True, you haven't cured a disease or solved world hunger, but you've done something well. Your home, your life—brand it as more organized and efficient. *Better*. For this, it's good to thank God.

In the common tasks of every day we can find ourselves at our most focused, disciplined, and poised as we work to move our lives forward. Keeping the shore in view and not drifting out to sea. This is about bringing skill and

dedication and, yes, love to the mundane. This is transforming the mundane into the meaningful.

Do you *love* every one of your daily tasks? Probably not. Most of them are no day at the beach. But can you do every task with love—love for a spouse, a child, and life itself? Yes. Can you do it with love for God, who makes it all possible? Yes. Most definitely, yes.

When we are present in the everyday moments, we find that God is present with us. And where God is, the flicker of a holy flame can help us see the commonplace in a whole new light.

Wherever your treasure is, there the
desires of your heart will also be.

MATTHEW 6:21

Relax, Rinse, Repeat

AT TODAY'S TRENDY beach spas, many clients like to start at the top: their hair. There's nothing quite like getting the spa hair treatment: The luxurious shampoo. The soothing scalp massage. The follicle-fortifying conditioning. The refreshing rinse. Maybe even the healthy "hair mask," made of natural ingredients like organic eggs and coconut. Ah, the joy of frolicking on the beach with your hair looking just right when it catches the breeze.

If spas charged by number of hairs, blonds would pay the most. If you are a blond, you sport approximately 140,000 hairs. If your hair is brown or black, you boast a respectable 110,000 or so. If you're a redhead, you own about 90,000 hairs atop your head, but, as gingers know, vivid equals volume.

The numbers above are only estimates, but God knows the *exact* number of hairs on your head. He loves you so much that it's important to Him to know the small details.

The psalmist David noted, "You know me inside and out, you know every bone in my body; you know exactly

how I was made, bit by bit, how I was sculpted from nothing into something. Like an open book, you watched me grow" (Psalm 139:15-16, MSG).

Like a deluxe, full-body spa treatment, God's love radiates from the bottoms of your feet to the top of your head—including every one of your thousands of hairs. Of course, your actual follicular total will vary from day to day. God's love does not.

The very hairs on your head are all numbered.
So don't be afraid; you are . . . valuable to God.

LUKE 12:7

Beach-Hot, or Not?

HOW WOULD YOU describe the perfect beach body? If you're a woman who has recently cringed after putting on your swimsuit, perhaps you should consider moving to Mauritania. In this West African country, it's believed that the more a woman weighs, the better her chance of securing a husband.

Meanwhile, along the border between Thailand and Myanmar, it's considered attractive to have a long neck. Really long. Women begin this "beauty treatment" as young girls by gradually stacking more and more heavy metal bands around their necks. By the time they reach adulthood, these women have weakened the muscles in their elongated necks so much that removing the bands would cause them to suffocate.

One might identify more with Western beauty standards, but even those have shifted dramatically over time. In 1700s America, pear-shaped figures were considered attractive for women. (So was shaving the eyebrows and

replacing them with brows made of press-on mouse skin.) In the 1800s, women were encouraged to look frail and pale. As for the men? Enter the fluffy powdered wig, which French King Louis XIV made popular in the 1600s when his hair started to thin at the ripe old age of seventeen.

When it comes to measuring one's worth, appearance is often part of the equation. For centuries, women and men have gone to extremes to meet the current criteria for physical charm and appeal.

But in reality, we're all different shapes and colors, each filling a unique spot—like a piece in a giant jigsaw puzzle that stretches through time. You may be an eye-catching crimson petal on a tulip or the emerald crest of an ocean wave.

Or you might be one of those pieces of blue sky. They all *seem* to look alike. But try to put one piece of sky into the spot designed for another piece, and what happens? You can try jamming it in or bending the corners. But even if you succeed in forcing that piece into a spot where it doesn't belong, it will never look right. And somewhere else in the puzzle there will be a spot where that now-mangled piece would have fit perfectly.

In a puzzle, every piece plays its part. In life, every person plays her or his part. Sometimes it takes a while to find your part. That's the adventure of being human— discovering what part of the Big Picture you were created to fill. It's like working a thousand-piece puzzle. That means you can feel free to try out for the community theater, see if playing guitar is your thing, or begin writing your blog.

If you're searching for a standard by which to measure yourself, be careful. Every time you compare yourself with another piece of the puzzle, you lose sight of how truly valuable that one-of-a-kind *you* really is.

If you must compare, compare who you are *trying* to be with who you believe you truly are in your heart. If something is off, ask God to show you the way. Ask Him to reveal the obstacles in your life. Ask for the wisdom and strength to overcome them.

He will help. Because He knows that no one can be a better you than *you*.

You made all the delicate, inner parts of my body
and knit me together in my mother's womb.
Thank you for making me so wonderfully complex!
Your workmanship is marvelous—how well I know it.

PSALM 139:13-14

God Is Stuck on You

THERE IS A good reason that some beach shops, spas, and high-end health food stores charge top dollar for sunscreens, shampoos, capsules, and lotions that support laminin health. You might not know it, but you are full of laminin. For this, you should give thanks. If not for laminin, you would be falling apart right now. And we don't mean having a freak-out. We are talking *actually* falling apart. Kind of like melting, à la the Wicked Witch of the West.

As the aesthetician at any beach spa might tell you, laminin is a vital protein. It's often called the body's superglue, and it helps hold your muscles, your skin, your eyes—all of you—together. It even keeps your hair from falling out.

God's love is a lot like laminin. It fills us up. It lives in every cell in our bodies, and it sticks to us, and with us, like the world's strongest epoxy. Even when life's stresses try to pull us apart, God's love inside keeps us strong. It holds us together, even when our world seems to be unraveling like a cheap sweater.

God loves you to pieces, and all of your precious pieces are held together in the strength of His forever love. Rest in this assurance. Bask in it. Then let this Good News stick with you wherever you go.

> *I am convinced that nothing can ever separate*
> *us from God's love. . . . Nothing in all creation*
> *will ever be able to separate us from the love*
> *of God that is revealed in Christ Jesus.*
>
> ROMANS 8:38-39

The Mystery of the Spirit Wind

LATE ONE AFTERNOON, a warm gust of wind stirs the ashes of a dying campfire—causing a glowing ember to pop into flame. The wind moves on, swishing through leaves on the trees beyond. Their branches dance.

Next, the wind shifts and floats back toward the nearby sea, whipping up high waves and rocking boats like cradles. Close to the seashore, a young boy feels the wind at his back. He stoops down and plucks a dandelion from the tall seaside grass, then blows gently on the fluffy white top. The seeds take off in the wind, drifting like tiny parachutes. Along the beach, the boy's sister and mother launch a kite into the wind. The kite rises, soars, and dips—like a crazy bird.

Later, as they walk home, the brother and sister talk about the amazing wind. They couldn't see the wind, but they could see how it moved the boats and the kite and the seeds. They could smell the scent the wind brought with it—the damp, sweet smell of the sea. They could feel the gentle way it ruffled their hair.

"God's Spirit is like the wind," their mother chimes in. "You can't see His Spirit, but it does so much work. We can see the results of that work all over the world—and in each of your little hearts. In bigger hearts too."

"Hearts like yours?" the girl asks.

"I hope and pray so" comes the reply.

They continue on their path and gaze at the squawking seagulls overhead, soaring on the invisible currents.

We, too, can soar . . . on the winds of grace and love.

The wind blows wherever it wants. Just as
you can hear the wind but can't tell where it
comes from or where it is going, so you can't
explain how people are born of the Spirit.

JOHN 3:8

Getting Away from It All (Far, Far Away)

ONE OF THE best things about beaches is how they help us "get away from it all," sometimes literally. Many of us gobble miles of highway or skyway to make our beach escapes. Among well-heeled American beach lovers, Japan's 1,300-year-old *onsen* spas are trendy right now, as are the spas located in Aidipsos, Greece.

Actually, those natural Aidipsos "hot spas" have been trendy for a long time and have attracted everyone from Aristotle to Winston Churchill to Greta Garbo.

One distinctive of the Greek spas: Their hot springs are located under the sea, allowing visitors to swim surrounded by the swirling bath-like waters. Imagine Aristotle, Plutarch, or Churchill dipping below the surface to seek refuge and solace, cheeks puffed out as they frog kick through the warm Grecian sea.

There are thousands of beach spas around the world,

but there will never be one in the Pacific Ocean just off the island of Guam. There you will find the Mariana Trench—a giant ditch, of sorts, on the ocean floor. The trench is almost seven miles deep. You could put Mount Everest in the bottom and its peak would still be more than a mile underwater.

If someone put a destination spa at the bottom of Mariana, you would need a specially built submarine to handle the great pressure of the water. Otherwise, you'd be squashed like a grape. Mariana's waters are not therapy.

But even if you could get your hands on a submersible, it would take five hours to get to the trench's bottom. And you would be praying the whole time that it wouldn't spring a leak.

In the Bible, we are promised that when we turn to God, He forgives our sins and sinks them to the ocean's bottom. So the next time you miss the mark, picture God taking your sin, letting it sink for miles, and then burying it in the bottom of the Mariana muck. The water spa where sins go to die. Never to be held against you, never to hold you back from being the person God wants you to be.

That thing you did—yes, even *that* one—it's forgiven and forgotten. Dead and deep-buried. Rest in peace.

*You'll sink our sins
to the bottom of the ocean.*

MICAH 7:19, MSG

Thank God for Your Pod

FLORIDA BOASTS SOME of the best sites for dolphin watching. The beaches of Marco Island, Naples Bay, Fort Myers, and Sarasota are just a few great options. (If you can't make it to one of these dolphin-friendly beaches, google "beach cams" and do your dolphin watching from the convenience of your computer or mobile device.)

In the English language, clusters of critters are sometimes called by interesting names. We have packs of wolves and herds of sheep and murders of crows. Groups of dolphins are *pods*, and we can learn from them. They splash and play and perform entertaining tricks, kind of like a bunch of kids enjoying the beach.

More important, dolphins take care of their own. If one gets hurt or sick, two or more other dolphins form a "life raft" under their friend or relative and bring him to the water's surface so he can breathe.

Just as God provides dolphins with pods so they can care for one another, He has given us friends and family

and coworkers. Do we fully appreciate the blessing of traveling through life with so many people who support and care for us—in good times and in hard times?

How rough the waters of life would be without these angels on earth.

So among your prayers today, let one of them be this: "Thank God for my pod."

There are "friends" who destroy each other, but a real friend sticks closer than a brother.

Proverbs 18:24

Counting the Grains of Sand

HAVE YOU EVER stood on your favorite beach and wondered how many grains of sands it contains? If so, you are not alone. A team of British scientists is counting grains of sand on a Cornish beach in an effort to calculate the rate of coastal erosion. Researchers at Plymouth University are nearing the end of a five-year study, monitoring data from various instruments they have mounted on scaffolding at Perranporth Beach.

The final tally will soon be available. Any guesses on what it will be? Estimates indicate that just one cup of large-crystal sand contains over 30,000 grains, while a cup with somewhat smaller grains could number more than 80,000. That is a lot of sand grains. A lot of *anything*.

Now imagine this: Tomorrow morning you wake up and check your savings account balance. You discover that someone has deposited $86,400. You are sure it's a computer error—until the following day, when the same thing

happens. And the day after that, too. A daily dose of 86,400 portraits of George Washington.

Nice fantasy, huh? The truth is that you do have an account like this. Sort of. Label this account Time. Every morning, you get a fresh 86,400 seconds credited to you. Think of them as 86,400 grains of sand in your daily hourglass.

The catch, of course, is that the time you fail to use wisely is lost. With time, there are no carryovers.

Some people say that time is money.

Not so. You can't hoard time. You can't store it or borrow against it.

You use time or you lose it.

As you think about how to use your daily allotment of 86,400 seconds, remember . . .

You can't really manage time. But you *can* manage the things, people, and processes that take up your time.

Time is expensive. Business expert Lewis Timberlake estimates that 80 percent of the average businessperson's day is spent on things or people that yield only 2 percent of his or her results.

Time can't be saved for later use.

Time is a great equalizer. Everybody gets the same amount: popes, paupers, presidents, princesses, and pop stars alike. Success isn't about how much time one possesses; it's about how much time one *uses*.

Time is irreplaceable. "Making up for lost time" is a fantasy.

Time is ruled by priorities. You have enough time for just about anything—as long as that anything ranks high enough on your list. Mind your days. Note whether low-priority busywork or interruptions are robbing you time-blind.

How many times have you heard someone say, "Oh, if only I had more time!" (Especially on the last day of a beach vacation?)

How many times is that "someone" you? Be careful that you aren't deceived. The president of the United States has no more time than you do. Rich or poor, young or old, God gives everyone a possibility-rich twenty-four hours every day. How you spend those 86,400 seconds reveals what truly makes you tick.

Make the most of every opportunity
you have for doing good.

EPHESIANS 5:16, TLB

A Workout with a View

RUNNING ON THE beach is a worthy workout. It has many purposes, most centered on keeping hearts strong, muscles toned, and guts flat. Okay, flatish.

But there is more to running on the beach than what shows up on your fitness app. The next time you run, walk, waddle, or wheel on the beach, celebrate simply being *alive*. Celebrate motion. Release the thoughts and prayers that otherwise might burst inside. Exercise more than your body: Express your mind. Unleash your passion. Free your caged spirit.

Drink in the beauty around you and inside you. This is stretching the brevity of life. This is uniting the spirit and the body. Your soul is more than a tired little engine powering a doomed corpse. You are created in the image of *God*.

A romp on the beach is a song. Feel the sugar-sand. Marvel at the waves. Smile at the children. Forget, for the moment, the past. Stop, for the moment, your fixating on

the future. Be fully alive right now. Savor this moment like the last bite of your favorite meal.

There is always something beautiful about right now. Please don't miss it. Run, move, to embrace it.

A heart at peace gives life to the body.

PROVERBS 14:30, NIV

Beach Oxymora

HERE ARE A few of our favorite beach-related oxymora:

Jumbo shrimp
Plastic glasses
Working vacation
Advanced Beginner swimming class
All alone
Sun-shade
Ocean management
Weather expert
Minor sunburn pain

Can you identify with any of the above? Think we missed a good one or two—like "waterproof clothing"?

Here's one that certainly applies to the beach—and many other places as well: worship time.

Our dad is a pastor, so he uses terms like "worship hour," but he always taught us that worship should be a way of life. "If you're breathing," he said, "you can be worshiping."

This is especially true for the beach. You can't schedule time for worshiping, for pondering nature. Wonder doesn't arrive according to a schedule. Neither does spiritual insight nor awakening.

When you are blessed enough to enjoy the wonders of nature in some amazing place, don't get in amazement's way. *Allow* wonder. Wait for moments and insights that will bring you joy and wisdom and love.

Don't merely think about that fresh sea wind on your face and friendly sun at your back. Feel them . . . for as long as it takes.

Step beyond life's arbitrary boundary lines. Hide your timepiece, or at least ignore it. Live your life—your worshipful life. At the beach . . . and everywhere.

Since we are receiving a Kingdom that is unshakable,
let us be thankful and please God by worshiping
him with holy fear and awe.

Hebrews 12:28

Burning the Beach Burgers

EVERY NOW AND then, a new commercial appears, trumpeting the virtues of the latest technology in nonstick outdoor cookware. Who knew that a simple skillet could be "revolutionary!"? According to one online ad we saw, there are now skillets and pans so advanced that it seems one could cook glue in them and even *that* wouldn't stick.

After having a few beach cookouts ruined by burgers that refused to budge from our frying pan until they were reduced to ash-covered hockey pucks, we sprung for an outdoor cookware set featuring a "hard-anodized aluminum finish!" and the promise that "these pans are anti-abrasive and absolutely nonstick!" Because the Internet doesn't lie, right?

Here's the thing: The pans actually worked. Our kids called them the Miracle Pans. Our wives said they were truly foolproof. (And we knew which fools they were speaking of.)

But pans aside, we also know of some anodized Miracle People. Nothing bad seems to stick to them: No sadness.

No insult. No mistake. They seem impervious to everything negative.

Many of us, however, find that *everything* sticks. We try to get rid of that annoying crud, but it won't be scrubbed away, even with vigorous effort and industrial-strength cleansers.

Enter God. Did you know that we don't have to be spotless first before we come to Him? We don't have to pretend, *There's nothing wrong here! Nothing bad is stuck to me!*

God meets us where we are—on the top of a sunny beach dune or in the pits of despair. We don't have to get to a certain point on our spiritual path before He will show up.

More important, God meets us *as* we are: With all the burnt-in sin and shame and insecurity. With all the scrapes and scratches, dings and dents.

Perhaps the apostle Paul said it best: "We have this treasure in jars of clay" (2 Corinthians 4:7, NIV). You can't oversell the importance of this imagery. Paul said jars of clay, not pure gold. Not space-age anodized alloys. Let's face it: We are not the most amazing containers on the market.

But inside we hold treasure.

May the brilliance and power of the treasure we hold inside give us purpose and love—no matter what might be sticking to us on the outside.

If you only look at us, you might well miss the brightness. We carry this precious Message around in the unadorned clay pots of our ordinary lives.

2 Corinthians 4:7, MSG

Ocean Baptism

A HAFER BROTHERS' beach walk at dawn. Our prayer—"Show us . . . show us who You are and what we're missing." A most dangerous prayer, but a prayer most necessary.

Indeed, one lifetime cannot satisfy the hunger to explore and discover. We have time to turn only a few crisp pages of the Book of Wonder called Life. Moreover, truth cannot be wrestled into submission—you might as well wrestle an ocean wave. You end up sore and bewildered.

We walk. Waves romp in, spattering the cocoa sand with foam.

Moments later, we stumble upon a few souls standing in the damp sand. Two older ones sit on beach logs.

They are watching a silver-haired man and a wraith of a woman in the waist-deep water. The sea is like a vast, rolling sky: It is boundless, unraveling for miles. You can plunge into its depths, but it remains a great mystery.

The man speaks a few words that, from a distance, seem to disappear into the salt air. We move closer, quiet

as a prayer. The man's hand coils under the woman's swan neck. He lowers her gently, as if she is made of crystal.

Then she lifts from the sea, water beading on her forehead. Every drop is transparent but filled with invisible hurts, regrets, and sins of the past. They slide down her arms, off her hands, and into a vast ocean of grace. The woman steps into the embraces of her angels-on-earth.

A circle forms, hand in hand in hand. We wait for a benediction, but the silver man is silent. Because what speech could explain this moment? Grace does not always need to be explained. Sometimes, it just is.

In baptism we show that we have been saved from death and doom by the resurrection of Christ.

1 PETER 3:21, TLB

Table of Content

ON A WARM summer afternoon, an expert wood-carver sat surrounded by his creations on the front porch of his beach cottage, sipping lemonade and enjoying the view. An almost-finished carving of a manatee, looking as if it were gliding across the ocean floor, rested on his worktable.

When a friend stopped by for a quick visit, he was surprised to see the artisan relaxing. "It's only 1:30 in the afternoon," the friend observed. "Isn't it a little early in the day for a break? That manatee carving is exquisite, but don't you want to finish it right away?"

The artisan swallowed a mouthful of lemonade. "No break," he answered. "I'm done for the day." He pointed to the manatee. "My hands are sore. My eyes are tired. I want to be at my best when I finish him."

The friend, a young marketing executive, was puzzled. "What do you mean? It's too early in the day for you to stop carving. If you carve more figures, you can make more money. You could even hire an assistant to help you. You

could buy new tools. You could buy a shop so you wouldn't have to carve here at your cottage. You could rent it and make a fortune!"

"Why would I want to do that?" the carver asked.

"So you can make more money!" his friend sputtered.

"What would I do with all the extra money?"

"Why, enjoy life, of course!"

The carver took another sip of lemonade and gazed out at the ocean. He closed his eyes, locking in the memory. Then, drifting off to an afternoon nap, he mumbled contentedly, "Enjoy life? What do you think I'm doing?"

Life provides an abundance of blessings every day, and many are very close at hand. Let's ensure we don't get too busy to enjoy them.

True godliness with contentment is itself great wealth.

1 TIMOTHY 6:6

Putting Proof into Promises

"YOU CAN HAVE a body that will turn heads at the beach—in just thirty days, guaranteed!" Cue the eye roll, the weary sigh, and the sarcastic "Yeah, *right!*"

For us, the only heads turning at the beach are probably thinking, *Those are the whitest white dudes I've ever seen. Is there a mime convention in town?*

At this point in the twenty-first century, promises and guarantees are not what they used to be. We've all been burned too many times. We've seen that words, no matter how forcefully they are uttered, can be hollow.

Your manager or your mayor says, "I guarantee it."

You counter, "Prove it."

No wonder God's guarantees, God's promises, rise above the noise. They have substance. It's certainly no accident that so many of God's promises have been accompanied by tangible (and quite memorable) signs and wonders: Moses' burning bush. Aaron's budding rod. David's five smooth

stones. And let's not forget the rainbows—thousands of years' worth of rainbows.

When God makes guarantees, He proves that He means business. The God who loves us is the same One who sets the stars in the night sky, controls the rhythm of the tides, and follows winter with spring and night with day. As Scripture says, "The heavens declare the glory of God; the skies proclaim the work of his hands" (Psalm 19:1, NIV).

If only we will open our eyes, we can see all around us proclamations of God's might and declarations of His love.

Some Christians today observe seven sacraments (baptism, Eucharist, confirmation, reconciliation, anointing of the sick, marriage, and holy orders). Others only a few. Still others are simply not into what they call "that whole sacrament thing."

Maybe we are all wrong. Whatever we may choose to call them, our world displays hundreds of signs of God's steadfast commitment to care for His creation—a wealth of phenomena that can be *sacramental* if seen through holy eyes.

May you experience God's faithfulness in a thousand

ways and shapes: The comforting hug from a loved one. The melody of a favorite hymn. The sun setting behind the mighty ocean. Even the pages of a book. And remember always that *how* God shows His love is not as important as the life-saving fact that God *does* love. That's a guarantee we can always count on.

I've banked your promises in the vault of my heart.

PSALM 119:11, MSG

Listening to Ali

OUR FRIEND ALI is an ace lifeguard. She isn't an advanced lifeguard—she's the one who *trains* the advanced lifeguards. Her peers call her "the lifeguard the other lifeguards want to be saved by."

If you catch a cramp out in the surf, drift into a rip current, or have an unpleasant encounter with a Portuguese man-of-war, you want Ali or a lifeguard like her nearby.

We have been nearby when Ali has taught swim and lifeguard classes, and we have learned more than water safety and swimming techniques from her. One class was especially memorable—she was teaching a group of lifeguards, and the class didn't seem to be going well. Most of the pupils had their eyes fixed on their smartphones. A few fidgeted nervously, as if they had sand in their shorts. (To be fair, perhaps they did.)

The one student who was actually looking at Ali was being, to our eyes, overtly rude. She often shook her head vigorously or frowned at some of Ali's comments.

When the class ended, we were quick to console Ali: "Sorry your class was so rude. Especially that one girl. She seemed to disagree with almost everything. You should have called her out."

Ali smiled. "I disagree," she said. "That 'rude' girl? She was the *only* one listening! I teach a lot of these classes. Most people don't pay any attention to me. Others can manage only partial attention. But someone who listens to every word? That's a treasure. I think listening is a fine art and a wonderful personality trait. I value people who listen, even when they disagree with me. If you are disagreeing with me, at least you are thinking about what I am saying."

Amen, Ali. You just saved us—from ignorance.

If you quit listening, dear child . . .
you'll soon be out of your depth.

PROVERBS 19:27, MSG

Small Moments Matter Big-Time

MAGIC MOMENTS—YOU'VE HAD them . . .

Chugging a cold bubbling soda after an energetic game of beach volleyball. Holding a child's hand on a walk to the lakeshore ice cream shop. Casting your line from a favorite fishing pier. Seeing that familiar smile flash across your best friend's face when you meet up to spend time together. Hearing a relative mention *your* name when thanking God for sending His blessings.

Every moment like one of these is a gift to you from God. Our Creator sends them to remind us that His supply of love and kindness will never run out. And because of this, we should always be thankful.

These gifts also remind us to keep our eyes, minds, and hearts open to receive the blessings—both large and small—that await us in the future. Who knows what divine moments will fill our hearts with laughter and make us want to shout with joy?

God will load your world with blessings of myriad sizes

and shapes. Take time to enjoy them all. Delight in the good that's close at hand. Take time to do what you love, with the ones you love.

> *No eye has seen, no ear has heard,*
> *and no mind has imagined*
> *what God has prepared*
> *for those who love him.*
>
> 1 CORINTHIANS 2:9

The Best Beach in the World

IF YOU WANT to spark a fierce debate among lovers of sand and surf, just float this question: Which beach is best? According to *Condé Nast Traveler* magazine, the El Nido region of Palawan Island in the Philippines boasts the top beach. TripAdvisor says it's Grace Bay, located in the Turks and Caicos Islands of the Caribbean Sea. In the eyes of *U.S. News & World Report*, Seven Mile Beach in the Cayman Islands is the boss of beaches.

You might have another favorite. Bowman's Beach on Sanibel Island, Florida, perhaps? Or Anguilla's Rendezvous Bay?

Some people love to explain why their beach is best. But getting a sand-and-surf-and-shells lecture about the Bukit Peninsula isn't the same thing as being moved or inspired by it.

Likewise, as Christians, we often want to influence our friends, family, and coworkers who don't share our faith. Thus, we collect evidence, counterarguments, Bible verses,

proof texts, and all manner of tools to unleash the next time the opportunity arises. We are full of explanations. We are wired for witnessing.

Unfortunately, you can *win* a debate about God and *lose* a chance to draw someone to Him. Many a Christian has laid out an airtight case for her faith, only to hear, "I don't care about all of that. I don't believe in God, no matter what you say about Him. I just don't want to be a Christian."

Faith is often more about the will than the intellect. Jesus didn't say, "I will outdebate everyone so they will have no choice but to believe in me." He said, "I will *draw* everyone to myself" (John 12:32, emphasis added).

It's unlikely that a war of words would draw someone to faith—or spark a major life change. But we can each do our part to bring others to our Savior: Love one another. Forgive one another. Work to gain heavenly approval, not mere human approval. Be humble. Be a peacemaker. God has promised to bless you, peacemaker.

People can argue over apologetics, but who can argue with a life lived Jesus' way and the impact it has? That kind

of living has a way of drawing people in the right direction,
like the moon draws the tides.

*Be kind to one another, tenderhearted, forgiving one
another, as God in Christ forgave you.*

EPHESIANS 4:32, RSV

Your Solid Rock

IMAGINE A HUGE rock that rests on the shore of a mighty sea. Time and time again, the sea's huge waves splash over and against the rock, but the rock holds firm. It doesn't budge a millimeter.

During summer, the fiery sun beats down on the rock. Some of the wildflowers nearby wither and die, but the sun doesn't bother the rock one bit.

Fall brings downpours of rain. The rain and wind wash away litter that has collected near the rock. But the rock doesn't move.

In wintertime, the sea turns bitter cold. In some places, its waters turn to ice, hard as stone. But the rock stays . . . well, a rock.

Imagine, too, a brother and sister. Let's call them Dwayne and Desiree. As small children, they loved to play on the rock. They climbed it and danced on top. Sometimes they gathered their friends, and all of them pushed against the rock as hard as they could. The rock didn't even wiggle.

When storms came, Dwayne and Desiree hid near

the rock. It protected them from the lashing winds and hailstones.

Over the years, Dwayne and Desiree changed. Instead of jumping and playing on the rock, they enjoyed sitting on top and talking about life.

One day, they pondered how God was like a huge rock that had been part of their lives for a long time: Solid. Always there. Nothing can push Him around or change Him. You can depend on Him, because He will always be there for you.

On those stormy days, He is your shelter.

And on those beautiful and calm days, He allows you to look out at your world from a higher place—a place of vision and strength and hope.

I love you, LORD. You are my strength.

The LORD is my rock, my protection, my Savior.
My God is my rock.
I can run to him for safety.
He is my shield and my saving strength, my defender.

PSALM 18:1-2, NCV

A Shell of Yourself?

ONE OF THE best parts of a day at the beach is picking up seashells. What is a trip to the beach without having a few shells to bring home? Of course, most of the shells we pocket are broken. That's what happens when you are pummeled by rocks and waves and fumbled along the sea floor.

Perfect shells are rare—it's a novelty to find one.

But broken shells are more interesting, in myriad ways: You can see the layers that make up the whole. And the shapes! Stars, slices, and shards. Some look like uncut diamonds.

And how fabulous is it that every trip to the beach brings a new harvest of shells? Even the *same* beach just one day later will offer up a new menu.

So many lessons are here to glean for us shell pickers, us beachcombers.

First, God loves us as we are: Broken and beaten and shattered. All together or in parts and pieces, bearing all the signs of the struggle that is life.

What's more, every day we get to start a new search for treasures that are subtly hidden in this thing called life. What we find might not meet our expectations—it might not look exactly like what we had hoped for. But "not meeting" expectations can also mean exceeding them if we look hard enough. We must keep our eyes open.

Finally, you don't need to look whole and perfect to be beautiful. Moreover, you don't have to be whole and perfect to be interesting. Or helpful to others. Or cherished by God . . . who will one day make *all* things whole.

Accept one another, then, just as Christ accepted you.

ROMANS 15:7, NIV

Beach Rules

THE SIGN WAS titled "Beach Rules." We thought it was going to be one of those fun signs, with admonitions like "Don't be crabby" and "Be a happy clam."

Uh, no.

No food or beverages. No exceptions!
Do not swim alone. Do not swim after dark.
No dogs of ANY kind.
No volleyball, baseball, football, or soccer. [We were undaunted by this one, as we had come to play Australian Rules Football.]
No Jet Skis, motorboats, or motorized crafts of any kind.

And so it went. We read through the list of Beach Commandments. The last one made us smile: "Above all, have FUN!"

Right.

–

The sign's beach buzzkill got us thinking: Why is the Bible jam-packed with *Thou shalt nots*? Is God some kind of egomaniac who created people just so He could push them around? Wouldn't life be more pleasant without all those commandments?

Then again, why doesn't a mother let her toddler touch a hot stove? Why doesn't a teacher let his kids spend recess on a busy street instead of the playground? Why does a doctor insist on having a patient's medical history before she prescribes medication?

A toddler *wants* to touch the stove because the orange glow is alluring. Schoolkids might want to play in the street because the same old playground has become boring. And a sick person wants medication right now!—that background stuff is just more red tape.

At the moment that someone in these situations collides with a brick wall called "Rules," the first instinct is to get around, over, under, or through it.

Little thought is given to the fact that the rules are meant to protect, to ensure safety and happiness.

Similarly, abiding by our Creator's commandments

ensures our protection, fulfillment, peace, and well-being. The quality of our lives is a product of our choices, and we don't always have the information, wisdom, or perspective to make the *best* choices. That's precisely why the God who loves us and yearns to see us succeed has given us rules to live by.

Besides, at their core, even the commandments that begin with "Don't" or "Thou shalt not" are *positive*. For example, "Don't covet" is another way of saying "DO appreciate what you have. Get true joy from it by avoiding comparing your stuff with someone else's."

"Don't kill" means "DO value and treasure life—both yours and the lives of others. DO realize that God created every person with the capacity to do good in the world. Be aware that maliciously robbing another human being of his or her life, potential, and dreams is inherently evil."

If you have been viewing the Ten Commandments or other biblical rules as a big stick God uses to beat His creation into submission, it's time to shift your perspective. God is for you, not against you.

How blessed you are to have a Lord and Savior who

cares enough to provide rules that will help you achieve the "abundant life" Jesus promised.

*Your word is a lamp to guide my feet
and a light for my path.*

PSALM 119:105

Bad Birds

WHAT ARE THE most annoying birds on the beach? In Florida, people often say the seagulls. In Southern California, it might be the LAPD helicopters. But at resorts like Monkey Beach in the Canary Islands, folks are peeved at the pigeons: The pigeons who chortle nonstop. The pigeons who dive-bomb and steal food. The pigeons who do other forms of "bombing" we won't discuss here.

Here's some information we hope will help you view those pigeons with less malice: They have actually helped win wars and save lives. In World War II alone, some fifty-four thousand carrier pigeons were "enlisted" in the US Army's Signal Corps. Their job? Transmitting critical information gleaned from soldiers on the front lines.

Many of these pigeons, bearing fond names like Pepperhead, Holy Ghost, and Blackie, were heroes in their own right. Consider what happened on October 18, 1943: American forces had called for an attack on the town of Calvi Vecchia, Italy. But in a sudden turn of events, the occupying German troops retreated and the British 56th Infantry moved in. Unless this news quickly reached the Allied bombers, the

Brits would soon become victims of friendly fire. Tensions rose as radio communications somehow failed.

Enter GI Joe.

Not your ordinary GI Joe—the winged variety.

This remarkable pigeon flew twenty miles in twenty minutes to deliver the critical message to abort the mission. According to one soldier, if GI Joe had arrived five minutes later, "the story might have been different." For his valiant effort, the British conferred on GI Joe the Dickin Medal for Gallantry—an award honoring the work of animals in military conflict.

So the next time a bird steals that last bite of your sandwich at the beach, don't get into a flap. Think of GI Joe and remember—not all birds are bad. Jesus even used them for an object lesson: How much more will our Father in heaven take care of you if He faithfully feeds the birds of the air? Granted, He may use your sandwich to do so. But according to His promise, don't worry! He'll more than make it up to you.

Look at the birds. They don't plant or harvest or store food in barns, for your heavenly Father feeds them. And aren't you far more valuable to him than they are? Can all your worries add a single moment to your life?

MATTHEW 6:26-27

Risking Your Life for Bird Spit?

WHAT WOULD YOU be willing to risk for a little bit of bird spit?

Your life savings?

Your life?

Don't answer too quickly.

Thailand's six Phi Phi Islands are home to some of the world's best beaches. Long Beach, for example, offers calm emerald waters and sand like powdered sugar.

On the "world's best beaches" lists, Long Beach often cracks the top ten. But there is more to the Phi Phis than beaches. Here, in fact, you will find some of the world's most unusual treasure hunters.

The Phi Phis have limestone cliffs that rise from the sea, some of them taller than a skyscraper. The treasure hunters risk their lives climbing these cliffs, via wobbly bamboo scaffolding, in search of White Gold.

This White Gold is not a precious metal . . . it's the spit of a type of bird called a swiftlet.

In an unconventional twist of nature, these birds use

spit to make their nests. The treasure hunters gather as many nests as they can in order to sell them to customers like restaurants, who use them to make soup. Now mind you, in our humble opinion, swiftlet spit looks and feels like Elmer's glue. But it doesn't taste like it. (And, yes, we know what glue tastes like. Don't judge.)

If someone offers you a bowl of "Bird's Nest Soup," beware. The price is nothing to spit at. One bowl can cost sixty bucks. Oftentimes more.

Why so expensive?

Many believe that swiftlet spit is a miracle elixir, helping the old to feel young and strong and the wheezing to breathe freely. And White Gold is said to ward off disease like a ferocious watchdog. Thus, those bamboo-climbing treasure hunters can sell their nests for thousands and thousands of dollars. For them, bird spit is indeed a precious treasure.

This brings us to a question: What do *you* treasure? What inspires your death-defying climbs in life—even the metaphorical ones?

We can all be treasure hunters every day. We can seek

God and the riches He wants us to have. Phi Phi's workers sometimes climb and search in vain, but God promises that everyone who looks for Him will find Him. And that's no spit.

There is treasure in the house of the godly.

PROVERBS 15:6

Coffee with Jesus?

ONE OF OUR favorite things about a morning walk on the beach is the beverage of choice: coffee. Home brewed or grabbed at the drive-through, coffee is essential to morning beach time. Sipping a hot coffee while watching the sunrise is a spiritual experience.

Or perhaps the previous sentence is hyperbole. After all, Jesus didn't drink coffee, did He?

We researched that question, and here is our answer: Probably not.

The term *coffee* derives from the Arabic word *qahwa*, which some sources say translates to "that which prevents sleep." People did not begin roasting coffee beans to create a beverage until the early thirteenth century, hundreds of years after Jesus walked the earth.

However, coffee plants did exist in Jesus' day—in northern Africa and the Middle East. And long before anyone thought of turning beans into beverage, resourceful people were mixing coffee beans (sometimes called coffee berries or cherries for their red color) with animal fat to create an early form of energy bar.

So while Jesus did not drink coffee, it is possible that He *ate* coffee!

Today, of course, coffee is as much a part of some church services as the bulletins, the pianos, and the little pencils. Many of the 2.25 billion cups of coffee consumed worldwide every single day (upwards of 400 million in the US) are enjoyed within the walls of a church. It seems that *qahwa* and life in the Spirit can complement one another, like coffee and cream.

But not all vital spiritual awakenings occur during a sermon. Sometimes, God will reveal Himself during a walk on the beach with someone you love—and a beverage you love. Soft sand and hard truths. Cool surf and warm fellowship. Coffee, cappuccino, café mocha . . . and the King of kings.

God is Spirit, so those who worship him must
worship in spirit and in truth.

JOHN 4:24

When Nothing Is Something

ANY HAFER TRIP to the beach is typically filled with important and impressive achievements. For example, we always strive to devote time to . . .

Listening to the wild, lost cries of birds way out at sea and trying to guess their provenance.

Tramping through wet sand to see what we think is a turtle or some other exotic marine animal near the shore. It's usually a rock.

Staring for a long time into a still tide pool. It's like a mirror of paradise itself.

Gazing at fat, drifting clouds that look like the faces of bearded old warriors.

We close no deals. We make no money. We solve no problems, local or global. We do no work.

And we are not sorry, for this we emphatically do: We find much joy. We entertain many pleasant thoughts. We

discover there are days when it is well to simply let the quiet peace of nature completely fill and heal the soul.

Tranquility is an achievement. Achieving tranquility is burying despair. For tranquility and despair cannot walk hand in hand, on the beach or anywhere.

A peaceful heart leads to a healthy body.

PROVERBS 14:30

Flunking the Beach Devotional

ONE OF OUR favorite beach devotional messages begins with a quick test. Or at least it should be quick, since it's a one-question test: List the five best sermons you have ever heard.

We recently posed the question to a pack of teens during a weekend campout at a southern Colorado reservoir. How do you think they did? (How would *you* do?)

Every teen flunked. And many of them were honor students. A few kids remembered a lesson or two—usually the most recent ones they had heard. One of them noted, "I really liked this one sermon about Jesus . . . and God."

Seeing we had frustrated our audience (as usual), we attempted to make things easier: "Okay, let's try a different approach. Forget about the *best* sermons. Just list ANY five you can remember."

Do you think that helped?

Nope. Everyone still flunked.

We collected all the test papers and tore them up. Then we handed everyone a new sheet of paper.

"This time, please list the five people who rank highest in importance to you—the ones who love you and help you the most."

How do you think the kids did this time?

Yes, everyone aced it. It was easy to make a list of important, helpful, and loving people. Some kids wrote more than five names. Some had ten. Others listed twenty or more. Moms and dads made the list. Foster parents. Grandmas and grandpas. Teachers, coaches, and babysitters. Even some sisters and brothers. Quite a few dogs and cats made the list too. Oh, and one gerbil.

We didn't give the kids that first test to make them feel bad. Instead, we wanted them to discover and understand that *people* are important.

People show us how God's Word works in the real world—what faith looks like. They are living sermons.

Remember to always be thankful for the good people God has placed in your life. Strive to be the kind of person who makes others' lives better and happier. Be a sermon. Better yet, be a servant.

As God's chosen people, holy and dearly loved,
clothe yourselves with compassion, kindness,
humility, gentleness and patience.

COLOSSIANS 3:12, NIV

Three Steps on the Beach

"WHAT THAT KID just did oughta be against the law!"—yeah, you can be pretty sure *that* was an exclamation uttered around the world when the news broke about eleven-year-old Thomas Gregory.

What Thomas did was shocking and set a world record that has never been broken—and never will be. Several years after Thomas completed his amazing adventure, new rules were established mandating that a boy or girl must be at least sixteen to make the attempt.

What did Thomas Gregory do one September day in 1988?

He swam all the way from France to England, knifing his way across roughly thirty-two miles of angry waters known as the English Channel. The feat has killed its share of strong adult swimmers. All told, only about one in ten adults who have attempted it has completed the swim. Olympic champion swimmers have tried and failed.

Keep in mind the host of other unpleasantries faced

by those braving the Channel: raw sewage, toxic oil slicks, painful jellyfish stings, and hungry, swirling whirlpools that enjoy nothing more than swallowing swimmers.

Along his epic journey, Thomas fought swelling waves as tall as Goliath. He punched through cramps in his arms, legs, and back. Hallucinations and near unconsciousness assaulted him. And all of this in water so cold that it felt like his blood was turning into a Slushie.

Thomas was not an Olympian or an early-blooming athletic freak. He looked like the slightly chunky middle schooler who lives down the street from you. He could still order from the kids' menu at local restaurants, yet he completed his swim in just under twelve hours, breaking his age group's record by almost three hours. He crossed the Channel in almost half the time of the first adult who officially made the swim—and that man had worn a special wet suit, the likes of which were later outlawed. Thomas's only protection was the tub of grease he applied on the bay beach just south of Calais, France, before plunging into the water at 5:15 a.m.

The boy's secret? He was determined to conquer what

many people consider the ultimate endurance challenge. That kept him going through hours-long training sessions in icy waters as he readied himself to face the Channel.

Many years later, he noted that he understood upping the age limit for Channel swimmers in order to look out for the welfare of children, but he added, "It's a shame if that gets in the way of what you call endeavor."

Before young Thomas's feat could become "official," he had to take three unaided steps on the beach at Dover, England. He dragged himself from the water, and he fell. He struggled to his feet. He collapsed again. And eventually . . . three wobbly steps to a world record.

Some of you reading this are oh-so-close to a goal that matters. Some of you will be that close someday.

Remember the stout preteen on the beach . . . the three faltering steps. You don't have to finish with flair. Just finish.

Anything is possible if you have faith.

MARK 9:23, TLB

Beach House

LOGAN WAS A skilled and loyal carpenter who had worked twenty years for a successful contractor. One day the contractor called Logan into his office and said, "I'm putting you in charge of the next house we build. It's going to be a cottage down by the beach. I want you to order all the materials and oversee the job from the ground up."

Logan enthusiastically accepted the assignment. He studied blueprints and double-checked the materials list, product specs, and measurements.

As he led the project, however, strange thoughts crept into his mind: *Hey, I'm in charge here, so I can cut a few corners if I want to. I can use cheaper materials, subcontract cheaper labor, and pocket the difference. Who will ever know? After all, I've worked hard for two decades—I deserve a little bonus.*

So Logan ordered second-grade lumber and inexpensive concrete. He installed cheap wiring and hired a few unskilled workers in his crews.

When the beach cottage was complete, the contractor

gave it a quick once-over. "Looks like a fine job as usual, Logan," he noted. "Now I have a surprise for you: You've been such a faithful carpenter for me all these years that I've decided to give you this cottage as your reward! I know you've always wanted to retire and live near the bay."

Build well today, whatever you're working on. Directly or indirectly, you will live with what you construct.

People with integrity walk safely,
but those who follow crooked paths will be exposed.

PROVERBS 10:9

True Treasure?

A FABLE . . .

A girl walked along the beach one day and spotted a new copper penny shining in the sand. She picked it up. A penny wasn't much, but it was hers. It had cost her nothing.

From that day on, she kept her head down whenever she was at the beach, closely scanning the sand for coins. Over the next decade, she collected 302 pennies, 24 nickels, 41 dimes, 8 quarters, 3 rare half-dollars, and a ragged paper dollar half-buried in the sand. The grand total: $12.82. Not a fortune, but *It cost me nothing*, she often reminded herself.

Or did it?

In her search for monetary scraps, she missed opportunities to gaze upon uncountable clouds floating overhead, colorful rainbows accenting stormy skies, and breathtaking sunsets filling ocean horizons. She missed seeing stingrays eject from the water and belly flop back into the blue. She missed hawks soaring and children splashing.

Acquiring isn't an inherently foolish act. It's all about *what* we acquire—and what we might miss during the process.

Teach us to live wisely and well!

PSALM 90:12, MSG

A Big-Fish Surprise, a Talking Donkey, and a Blazing Bush

IMAGINE THIS: YOU have applied your sunscreen, donned your shades, and settled into your favorite beach chair. You're finally ready to read that bestseller you bought last winter. (Or *pretend* to read while you nap in the sun, inscrutable behind your sunglasses.)

But at that moment, a mysterious sea beast surfaces near the shore, utters a painful moan, and spews a full-grown man onto your favorite beach towel: a prophet reeking of rotted seaweed and fish bile.

"You can call me Jonah," he says.

You're thinking, *More like Captain Beach Buzzkill. Or worse.*

We've always wondered what the people at the beach thought when Jonah arrived via the Giant Fish Express.

And we have always marveled at just how far God will go to talk with the people He created. Jonah is one of our favorite examples.

Of course, there are others . . .

When God wanted to grab Moses' attention, He spoke to him through a blazing bush.

When God wanted to help Balaam make the right choice, Balaam's donkey *talked*: a spokes-donkey, delivering an important message.

When God wanted the prophet Ezekiel to understand His plan to bring new life and hope to Israel, He turned a valley of old, dried-up bones into living people.

Is there any limit to what God will do to communicate, "Do I have your attention now?"

The attention-grabber supreme, of course, is Jesus. When God wanted to express His love for people everywhere—past, present, and future—He sent His Son to heal the sick, to show us how to live, and to die and take the punishment for our sins.

About 1,500 years later, God grabbed the attention of a Spanish knight after he was seriously wounded in battle. This knight is one of our favorite old-school saints, Saint Ignatius of Loyola. He was a fierce man of prayer, just as he

was a fierce warrior. He often spent seven hours a day communing with his Lord.

We want to close this piece with our own version of one of those prayers:

Lord Jesus, teach us to be generous;
teach us to serve You as You deserve—
to give and not to count the cost;
to fight and not to heed the wounds;
to toil and not to seek for rest;
to labor and not to seek reward,
except that of knowing that we do Your will.

The eyes of the Lord are on the righteous
and his ears are attentive to their prayer.

1 PETER 3:12, NIV

The Daily Grind

HOLLAND, MICHIGAN, IS home to some of our favorite beaches. The sands are golden, and the umbrellas that pop up in Holland State Park and along Ottawa Beach Road are almost as colorful as the city's famous tulips.

But Holland is famous for more than its flowers. For more than fifty years, the Lake Macatawa landscape has been crowned by DeZwaan, Holland's iconic windmill. (*DeZwaan* is Dutch for "swan" or "graceful bird.")

This fully functional windmill was built near Amsterdam in 1761. It survived World War II and was shipped to the United States after the city of Holland, in a tribute to its rich Dutch history, purchased it in the early 1960s.

The six-story marvel is the only authentic working Dutch windmill in the United States and is operated by Alisa Crawford, the only Dutch-certified female miller in the country.

Using two massive millstones weighing more than two and a half tons, DeZwaan produces flour from winter

wheat berries grown by west Michigan farmers. The stones are powered by wind-capturing blades measuring eighty feet long and six feet wide. From the gallery deck—which looks a bit like a ship's wheelhouse—the miller can turn the blades so they face into the wind or stop them from turning altogether.

Crawford tells us the ideal speed for turning the millstones is twenty to twenty-five miles per hour—a bit windy for a day at the beach, but just right in DeZwaan's wheelhouse. Literally.

The mill grinds about nine tons of grain annually, and the flour is sold locally and shipped worldwide. Many of Holland's beach eateries, downtown restaurants, and breweries use the whole wheat and graham flour for making pancakes, cookies, pizza crust, flatbreads, and much more. We can attest that almost nothing beats a DeZwaan-crust pizza after a long day at the beach.

Crawford talks about DeZwaan the way a parent brags on a child. When she describes hoisting fifty-pound bags of grain to the top of the windmill, setting the sails of the massive windmill blades, and sharpening the grindstones, she's describing not a job but a craft. A true labor of love. "History is so much more interesting when you live in it. Being inside this windmill . . . it's just too wonderful!" she says.

"Too wonderful." When was the last time you said that about your place of employment or the equipment used there?

At our little publishing enterprise, our printer doesn't care what it prints. The shredder cares not what it shreds, any more than our local butcher's meat grinder cares about the chorizo it's churning out. Machines, even wonderfully simple ones like DeZwaan, are indifferent toward their tasks. More bluntly, machines don't care. But every time we visit people like Alisa Crawford, we are reminded that the people who run the machinery do care, or at least they should. Through our love and passion for what we do, we surpass run-of-the-mill and are counted among the cream of the crop.

.

*Whatever you do, work at it with all your heart,
as working for the Lord, not for human masters.*

COLOSSIANS 3:23, NIV

A Picture of Peace

YEARS AGO, A woman created a watercolor painting. It showed her husband leaning into heavy winds and driving rains during a spring thunderstorm. In one arm, the man cuddled his baby daughter, using his big overcoat to shield her from the storm as he fought his way home, trudging through a lakeshore's soggy sand. Despite the storm, the baby was sleeping soundly. The woman titled her painting *Peace*.

Yes, *Peace*.

This wise artist knew that true peace—peace of the heart—isn't about dodging every problem or trouble. Peace is trusting a loving heavenly Father who is always with us. And He is especially close when life's storms rage all around.

We can experience more of God's peace when we . . .

focus on our all-powerful God, above and beyond anyone or anything else;

ask God for peace that will calm our hearts;

find someone to talk with us, listen to us, hug us, and
love us; and

find a poem or Bible verse to read and a song to sing
when we need an extra dose of God's peace.

Remember, God has promised to be with you always.
And wherever God is, His peace is there too!

*Where God's love is, there is no fear, because God's
perfect love drives out fear.*

1 John 4:18, NCV

Through the Maze

IF YOU'VE EVER visited Myrtle Beach, South Carolina, it's possible you made it to the ah-maze-ing Maze Mania.

Though not currently in operation, the 2.5-acre life-size puzzle served up a ton of fun while putting your navigational skills to the test.

Beat the best time of the day and you won a shirt. You could attempt the maze as many times as you liked—but with continually changing walls, success on Thursday meant nothing on Friday.

Many tourists did not have the mettle for Maze Mania. Eventually they threw their hands up in frustration, shouting, "Where am I, and how do I get out of this place?!" Mind you, they preferred not to ask for help . . . but they were lost—and getting "loster."

Above the Myrtle Beach maze sat an observation deck, where friends or family could offer guidance: "Keep turning right, and you'll be okay," they called. Or "You need to backtrack; you're headed for another dead end!"

Like a person in a maze, we don't always know which way to go. Today's route to freedom might be tomorrow's dead end. But God is above it all—He sees where we need to go and which paths we should avoid. This is why we must be willing to quit focusing on the confusion in front of us and call out to God instead.

There is a way out. God's mercies are renewed daily. Look to Him—you'll be amazed.

Seek his will in all you do,
and he will show you which path to take.

PROVERBS 3:6

For the Love of a Penny

PICTURE THIS: YOU'RE searching for shells and interesting marine life on the beach. But all you're finding is seaweed and soda cans. Then a shiny penny steals your attention. Do you stoop down to pick it up? That depends on how much it's worth to you. If you're feeling rich, why bother with that little coin? What's it going to get you—one piece of bubble gum? Not even. Not anymore. Besides, why should one coin hijack your beachcombing?

But what if your pockets were empty? What if you hadn't eaten since yesterday? In that case, a penny might seem like the beginning of something big.

Jesus sprinkled words of praise on a widow who gave a gift of two coins to the Temple. She wasn't the only one donating money that day. Many people—rich in earthly treasure—were dropping off fat wads of cash. But Jesus told His disciples this woman had given the biggest gift of the day.

Those disciples must have thought Jesus wasn't very

good at math until He offered an explanation: The wealthy benefactors had given a tiny fraction from their bank accounts. This woman had given 100 percent—all that she had.

Are you feeling like you don't have much to offer? Perhaps you don't, if we're talking about money. But you do have love. And probably good intentions and good ideas.

What can you do with them? Don't you have to start a big organization to make a difference? Furthermore, if you give just a few pennies to your church or an existing charity, can that really help someone?

It can, if those few pennies go to someone who needs them. Did you know that just sixteen cents can provide a healthful meal for a student in Kenya?

By the way, God loves it when you give those pennies because you *want* to, not because you feel like you should.

In the New Testament, the apostle Paul writes, "You must each decide in your heart how much to give. And don't give reluctantly or in response to pressure. 'For God loves a person who gives cheerfully'" (2 Corinthians 9:7).

God isn't impressed by how much money or stuff

you donate. To Him, generosity is measured by the size of your heart.

It might be your pennies, found on the beach or elsewhere. It might be your time, talent, toys, clothes. Whatever it is, God can use small gifts to do great things.

Whoever has the gift of giving to others should give freely.

ROMANS 12:8, NCV

"Worms on the Beach" with Charles Spurgeon

HERE'S A QUIZ for you: Why did famed circus pioneer P. T. Barnum invite nineteenth-century English minister Charles Spurgeon to tour with him? Answer: More than ten thousand people would flock to hear Spurgeon speak—at the age of twenty-two! Not surprising, we suppose, for a guy who started preaching at sixteen. (The minister took a pass on the tour, by the way.)

Spurgeon was also a beach guy. He walked popular ones like Ramsgate, but his preference was for smaller, more obscure sites without names. Describing one such beach, Spurgeon observed, "What hundreds of little mounds there are all over the beach, where the worms have come up and made a number of small heaps."

So a guy goes to the beach and focuses on *worms?* Yes. And there's more: "That is all we [humans] do, and it is all

that the world is, just a big place covered all over with little heaps of dirt that we have all piled up."

Observations like this didn't make Spurgeon feel hopeless. He drew inspiration from things like worms on the beach. He knew that the little things matter.

Spurgeon was also characterized by a deep compassion for orphans. He made great strides in caring for "the least of these" when he founded London's Stockwell Orphanage in 1867. But how would he fund such a bold endeavor? Although the charismatic young preacher wasn't a fan of the spotlight, he rightly leveraged his fame to provide the answer. Spurgeon spied a solution by organizing annual camp meetings that featured his classic sermons. Offerings received at the massive gatherings were used to feed, clothe, shelter, and educate some five hundred orphans.

In spite of such wonderful deeds, there were those who accused Spurgeon of reveling in his own popularity. Others, perhaps, envied the large sums of cash his offerings could bring in. It's said that after one particular collection, a man confronted Spurgeon and took him to task: "I had always heard you preached for souls, not for money." Spurgeon

stared at his critic. "Sir," he said, "usually I do preach for souls, but my orphans cannot eat souls. And if they could, it would take four souls the size of yours to make a square meal for just one orphan!"

Following this incident, his critics faded into the background. Score another victory for this warmhearted, cigar-puffing, God-fearing, eloquently spoken legend of a man, Mr. Charles Haddon Spurgeon.

After his death at the young age of fifty-seven, the Stockwell Orphanage continued to thrive. Now known as Spurgeons, its legacy of hope continues as a Christ-centered charity serving children and struggling families in the United Kingdom.

Some people build their "mounds on the beach" as monuments to self. Others build compassion and hope.

Use your freedom to serve one another in love.

GALATIANS 5:13

Go, Lemmings!

YOU PROBABLY WON'T find any actual lemmings on Lemmings Beach, Cyprus. They prefer colder climates.

Lemmings, as you might know, are small rodents who migrate in huge, furry masses. While lemmings do not plunge willy-nilly off high cliffs as some people believe, sometimes their "mass movement" approach leads to disaster, as when they try to swim across a large body of water, and those who aren't fit don't make it.

This is one reason there are no sports teams called the Lemmings. After all, who would want to be named after a crowd-following critter that sometimes swims its way to doom?

Let's face it: We all want to be part of the crowd sometimes. When we are part of the masses, we feel like we belong.

This is why Jesus is such a great and revolutionary example. He simply didn't care about being part of the majority, the in-crowd. He hung out with unpopular

people. And He wasn't afraid to stand alone, pray alone, even die alone.

We should always remember that our goal is to be faithful to Jesus, regardless of where our peers are headed. Choosing friends wisely is a great way to stay on track. Christian recording artist TobyMac says it this way: "You are who you roll with."

Diverting from the mass movement of the crowd is risky. Standing alone takes courage. It can bring ridicule and name-calling.

But at least one of those names won't be "Lemming!"

Don't copy the behavior and customs of this world, but let God transform you into a new person by changing the way you think. Then you will learn to know God's will for you, which is good and pleasing and perfect.

ROMANS 12:2

Uncommon-tary

MOST LIKELY, YOU began today in unspectacular fashion. Your own private robot didn't roll into your room and wake you by playing a selection of your favorite songs on his state-of-the-art sound system.

You didn't begin the day with a brisk workout with a live-in personal trainer—followed by a massage from your masseuse. A private chef didn't cook your favorite breakfast, complete with freshly squeezed orange juice and imported Swiss hot chocolate and pastries flown in from France.

When you head to the beach or lakeshore, your mode of transportation is not a stretch limo piloted by Ernest, your personal chauffeur. And you have to share your sand and sun with other beachgoers. You don't own a private island like Marlon Brando did way back when.

In short, your day—like your life—is rather common. But that doesn't mean it has to be boring or unremarkable. Every day, God provides dozens of treasures for those with eyes to see them and hearts to appreciate them: The

warmth of a friend's smile. The camaraderie of sharing a meal or a favorite TV show with family members. The glory of a sunrise. The beauty of a sunset over the water. The comfort of crawling into a warm bed after a busy day.

So the next time your life seems too dull, too common, look past the surface elements of life to the hidden delights. A common life can be uncommonly good.

[Jesus said,] "I tell you, do not worry about
your life, what you will eat or drink; or about
your body, what you will wear. Is not life more
than food, and the body more than clothes?"

MATTHEW 6:25, NIV

Thanks for Nothing

WE MISSED OUR day at the beach.

It's not that we failed to reach our destination. We arrived just fine, actually.

First we packed the car. Then made the drive. Unpacked the car. Staked out our slice of the beach.

We clocked time there—three hours and eleven minutes, to be precise.

But we missed the experience.

We missed the way the salt sea soothes the spirit and body—God's spa. We missed the spectacular show presented by the Pacific and the swaying palm trees—God's motion picture in 3-D! We missed the magic barefoot movement through the warm, wet sand—God's playground. We missed the caress of the gentle beach breeze—God's masseuse.

All because . . .

The drive on the interstate was a high-speed demolition derby. The beach was packed like the DMV at lunch

hour. The time was too short—almost everyone had "things to do" back home.

The beach was still there, in all its wonder. Yet we missed it—not because of all the distractions, really . . . but because we failed to give thanks. We failed to be grateful for the surf, the sand, and the kind sun.

Because of this, we have no good memories of our day at the beach. In fact, we have almost no memories at all, save for the heavy and sad reality that we missed the opportunity.

A psychologist we know informed us that when we fail to be thankful for experiences, our brain fails to register them as warm, life-giving memories. We believe that a lack of gratitude robs the soul as well as the mind.

C. S. Lewis said, "Gratitude is the key to happiness." Every day that we forget this tends to be a very bad day.

Please don't miss your day at the beach, or your day in the mountains, or your day at the family gathering. Don't miss your day at the . . . anywhere.

Give thanks. If you think you are too busy to thank God a few times a day, you should probably thank God *many* times a day—because, like us, you are missing out on the joy of living gratefully.

Stop thinking so much. Stop worrying so much. With thanks in your heart, jump into that water.

Cultivate thankfulness.

COLOSSIANS 3:15, MSG

Drastic Measures

YOU'VE PROBABLY EXPERIENCED it: Someone your age walks by on the beach, looking like a million dollars. Meanwhile, you're having one of those $9.95 days. A "woe is me—I don't measure up" episode.

Dollars, cents, millimeters, miles, cubic feet, cups, pounds, percentages, degrees, and decibels—if we're going to measure something, we need a standard.

Perhaps the same is true with our self-worth. If we're trying to figure out whether or not we matter, we need to understand how to assess a person's value, right?

According to *Wired* magazine, if a human body were sold for each of its individual parts—a brain, a liver, a kidney—the price could total $45 million. However, when the body is simply reduced to its basic elements and minerals, it rings up to about $160.

We've never been math aces, but it seems that money isn't a reliable measuring stick. Besides, whether we go for the high number or the low one, we're talking about how

much our bodies are worth once we're no longer using them—or at least parts of them. Using the bodies we're in right now to surf, kayak, run through the sand, or savor an ice cream cone while basking in the sun . . . how do you put a price tag on that?

Your value is not dictated by any person or institution, so it cannot be retracted. Value is not defined by humanity or machine. Our inherent, God-given sanctity trumps labels, grades, and rating systems.

Being a good husband, wife, parent, or friend is—to render an understatement—just as important as being a good president or movie star or business mogul, right? And it's *way* more important than how you look on the beach.

God loves you and values you. This is the truth, and we function most effectively when we walk in truth—because the truth sets us free.

God does not see the same way people see. People look at the outside of a person, but the LORD looks at the heart.

1 SAMUEL 16:7, NCV

A Froggy Day at the Lake

A PARABLE BASED on one of our dad's favorite sermon illustrations . . .

A group of frogs was hopping along a lakeshore. Suddenly, two of them plunged into a deep pit covered by loose grass and weeds. As the other frogs circled around, they quickly concluded that their amphibious friends were doomed. Frantically, the two unfortunate frogs began leaping with all of their strength.

"Give it up," their cohorts scolded them. "You are as good as dead!"

But still the two frogs kept jumping.

After a half hour, one of them became discouraged. He curled up in a dark corner and waited to die. Despite the continued jeers of his companions, the other kept at it. Finally, with one mighty lunge, he propelled his tired body to the top of the pit, barely grasping its rim, and pulled himself to safety.

"Wow—you sure have hops!" one of the spectators

shouted with surprise. "I guess it was a good thing you ignored our taunts."

The now safe frog looked at his companions, a puzzled expression on his green face. Then, using intricate sign language gestures, he explained that he was deaf. *Just now I could read your lips*, the frog signed, *but in the pit, I could only see your frantic gestures. I assumed you were encouraging me!*

What amazing things we can accomplish when we turn a deaf ear—or two—to those who don't believe in us.

Whoever mocks the poor shows contempt for their Maker;
whoever gloats over disaster will not go unpunished.

PROVERBS 17:5, NIV

Nothing Ever Happens on "Some Day"

DO ANY OF these statements sound like you?

> "Someday I'll take my family to the beach."
> "Someday I'll volunteer to do community service."
> "Someday I'll actually use my vacation days."
> "Someday I'll call or e-mail my old friend—as soon as
>   things get less crazy."

Good intentions are fine, but there is a problem with *someday* statements. Sometimes, "some day" never comes. Opportunities vanish. Kids grow up. Long-lost friends move (again) and fade out of your life.

Heaven knows that life can be busy. But it's *your* life, and it's up to you how you will spend it. Don't let opportunities to reach out and touch the lives of others slip through your fingers, like sand passing through an hourglass.

Make an effort. Set priorities. Give yourself time limits if you must. Send that letter or e-mail. Make that call. Buy that gift. Put your name on the volunteer list—get committed.

Do something kind for your neighbor while he or she is still a neighbor. Learn to surf. Then teach somebody else to surf.

Don't look at time as a prison. Think of it as a gift from God. Then as you sort through your life's priorities, think of how God wants you to use His gift of time. You will know the answer—not someday, but today.

Don't brashly announce what you're going to do tomorrow;
you don't know the first thing about tomorrow.

PROVERBS 27:1, MSG

Moomaw!

THE SHENANDOAH VALLEY is probably not the first area that comes to mind when you think of a beach vacation. But it should be on your short list. The valley and its national park are treasures for water lovers. We particularly love Lake Moomaw, located in the valley's southwestern region. Because it is a vast, 2,530-acre water playground. And because we love to say *Moomaw*.

One of our favorite artists created a wonderful oil painting of Shenandoah. Done in simple American Primitive style, the painting features a welcoming lake (we like to think it's Moomaw) surrounded by trees and farmland.

We also love the painting because it answers the question "How late is *too late* to make a major change in life and do something great—something that would make a difference in the world?"

Shenandoah Valley was rendered by a woman who decided to take up painting in earnest in her seventies. She had never taken a formal art lesson. In fact, she possessed

very little formal education—period—and had spent more than fifty years working on farms. Eventually arthritis made it difficult for her to continue her hobby of fashioning embroidery pictures.

So the septuagenarian decided to pursue painting.

Ten years later she was one of the best-known and best-loved artists in the world. By the time she reached ninety, the galleries displaying her work outnumbered the candles on her cake. And the icing on her one-hundredth-birthday cake? Making the cover of *Life* magazine.

This late bloomer passed away in 1961 at age 101. She had spent almost a quarter of a century as a world-class artist. Every major newspaper and newsmagazine in the country featured tributes and retrospectives. From across the world, various heads of state sent their condolences to her family.

Grandma Moses was her name.

When asked how she decided to become a painter, she said, "If I didn't start painting, I would have raised chickens." She thought about who she truly was, what she wanted to become, and how to get there. "Life is what we make it,

always has been, always will be," Grandma Moses reflected in her later golden years.

So the next time you fear it's too late to realize your dreams, think of Grandma Moses. The painting of your life isn't complete until you say it's complete.

Find your Moomaw.

"I know the plans I have for you," declares the LORD, *"plans to prosper you and not to harm you, plans to give you hope and a future. Then you will call on me and come and pray to me, and I will listen to you. You will seek me and find me when you seek me with all your heart."*

JEREMIAH 29:11-13, NIV

Finding Your Inner Heston

THE CHANCES ARE likely that at some point in your life, you've stood on the shore of a lake or ocean and thought about the parting of the Red Sea. Admit it. You stretched out your arms over the water and unleashed your inner Moses/Charlton Heston (or at least you wanted to).

When some people hear the word "God," they think of the Red Sea–parting, earth-shaking, raising-the-dead power behind the universe. Yes, this is God.

But God also revealed Himself in the form of His Son— a helpless infant born in a barn more than two thousand years ago. The next time you hold a baby in your arms, imagine the Ruler of the universe cooing with delight, crying in hunger, or shivering from the cold.

God could have come to earth as a fully mature adult or an invincible superhuman hero. But He deliberately chose to experience every stage of growth to adulthood. He knows firsthand what it's like to be a child, a teen, a young man.

God the Son probably endured his share of nightmares, bruises and scrapes, harassment from bullies, misunderstandings with his earthly parents, social isolation, and betrayal by so-called friends. And yes, Jesus even went through puberty.

No wonder the Bible is full of passages about how much God loves the younger members of His creation. He knows their struggles. Jesus empathized with them so much that he taught this important truth: "Anyone who welcomes a little child like this on my behalf welcomes me, and anyone who welcomes me welcomes not only me but also my Father who sent me" (Mark 9:37).

But while it's true that Jesus holds a special place in His heart for little ones, His love is equally strong for those of every age. The Savior is intimately acquainted with every heartache and joy known to humankind.

So the next time you find yourself facing a Red Sea, don't just think about God's awesome power. Whether you are young, old, or somewhere in between, reflect on the comforting truth that God understands, from experience, what it's like to be you.

He will rescue the poor when they cry to him;
he will help the oppressed, who have no one to defend them.
He feels pity for the weak and the needy. . . .
For their lives are precious to him.

PSALM 72:12-14

Zipping Up the Details

IT'S A COLD day at the beach—the season for light jackets and wind pants. As we're zipping up to escape the chill, three initials catch our eyes: YKK.

But they're not just on our jackets. We also find them embossed on our life vest zippers and ultralightweight "Hot-n-Cold" beach tote bag.

Chances are, you've seen those mysterious initials too. So what do they stand for already?

We'll divulge the info, but you must do the pronouncing: Yoshida Kogyo Kabushikikaisha—Japan's eighty-three-year-old zipper company.

There's a reason the YKK brand is so prolific, and we can sum it up in one word—quality.

Did you know that YKK's top-notch standards dictate keeping each stage of zipper making in-house? They smelt the brass, forge the zipper teeth, and spin the thread. In Japan, even the packaging that the zippers are shipped in is made on-site.

The more than one million miles of YKK zippers manu-
factured every year are used in products ranging from jeans
to fanny packs to expedition tents.

And portable beach-umbrella carriers.

We vest up and plunge into the refreshingly cold surf.
Yes, the vests are more than a decade old, but the zippers
still work great.

When we finish our swim, we scrawl "YKK" in the sand.
This cold day at the beach is a bit warmer—and we are
safer—because of three inconspicuous initials. And the fact
that people oceans away still care about the details.

Who dares despise the day of small things?

ZECHARIAH 4:10, NIV

A Passion for Compassion

IT'S NOT OFTEN that we see a beach lifeguard racing to the aid of a struggling swimmer or victim of some other emergency, but when we do, we say a prayer of thanks for a Civil War hero named Clara.

Of the many great women in American history, few are as admirable as Clara Barton. She began her career as a teacher at age fifteen—in 1836, when almost all teachers were men (and not teenage men).

Later in life, in her forties, she served as a nurse in the Civil War, sometimes risking everything in the heat of battle to tend to the wounded. Her courage, expertise, and grace earned her the title "Angel of the Battlefield." Clara didn't just tend to soldiers' wounds; she read to them, wrote letters for them, listened to their concerns and stories, and prayed with them. Her service continued after the war ended as she worked to reunite injured soldiers with their families.

In 1881, at age sixty, Clara founded the American Red

Cross, which she led for twenty-three years, never drawing a salary. The Red Cross was one of the first organizations to train people in aquatic lifesaving and resuscitation. Clara lived to see the first lifeguards employ their expertise and courage to save swimmers endangered by everything from riptides to jellyfish stings to broken bones.

The hallmark of Barton's life was compassion. This word comes from the Latin stems *com* ("with") and *pati* ("suffer"). Compassionate people suffer with others. They take others' pain and grief as their own.

Barton displayed her compassion at an early age. When she was eleven, her older brother David was seriously injured when he fell from the rafters while building a barn. For two years, Clara helped care for David, developing the skills and patience that would serve her on the battlefield many years later.

Even though she worked on some of the Civil War's bloodiest battlefields, she didn't feel that her service was anything extraordinary. "While our soldiers can stand and fight, I can stand and feed and nurse them," she said matter-of-factly. "You must never so much as think whether you

like it or not, whether it is bearable or not; you must never think of anything except the need, and how to meet it."

We can't all serve on the battlefield or start huge organizations. Not all can be lifeguards. But when we see the needs around us, we can still emulate Clara Barton by allowing compassion to fill our hearts.

Then we can share the hope of the Cross, red or otherwise.

Love one another,
be compassionate and humble.

1 PETER 3:8, NIV

A Friend in High Places
(Really, Really High Places)

THE WONDERS OF the beach don't fade at sunset. What can match stargazing on a clear night, with the music of the water as its backdrop?

Stargazing, of course, is a misnomer. The glow reaching our eyes is thousands of years old, meaning that many of the "stars" we watch from the sand are really just light-ghosts. Most likely, they have long since burned out.

You probably know that our sun is a star. It's big to us—but not so grand among its peers. One particular star in our galaxy's Eta Carinae stellar system outshines the sun the same way a huge forest fire outshines one small birthday candle.

And let's talk about the neutron star: If you could scoop just one spoonful of its matter, that bite would weigh as much as eight thousand aircraft carriers!

Can you wrap your brain around those amazing facts?

Consider an even greater mystery: The power behind such wonders is also at work in us who believe. The Bible puts it this way—"If the alive-and-present God who raised Jesus from the dead moves into your life, he'll do the same thing in you that he did in Jesus, bringing you alive to himself" (Romans 8:11, MSG). Indeed, we have access to God's astonishing power over sin and death—the highest force in a vast universe.

So whenever you gaze up at the sun or the nighttime stars, remember that God is your friend in high places. The same God who built the universe wants to show up in your life in stellar ways. Keep looking up.

I am the one who made the earth
and created people to live on it.
With my hands I stretched out the heavens.
All the stars are at my command.

ISAIAH 45:12

Night Light

IT'S LATE. THE sun has slipped away. The moon-kissed sea shines like obsidian. Only a few bright embers glow in our fire pit. They hiss in protest as we douse them with water from a dented bucket.

We look around, up, and out. We return to this world from some far-off place where our minds, our souls, have wandered. What time is it, anyway? Out here, there is no clock ticking with somber precision. One could walk up to the car and check, but that would take, what—two or three minutes? And to make that effort, we would have to care about what time it is.

So, instead, we walk through the sand and look across the still waters. The fat moon looms silver in the near distance. Behind us, the great dunes stand like sentinels. The tide slides in and erases our tracks from the shore.

We smile at our fresh, untracked world—dark, beautiful, and almost silent. It feels like unreality, but it's more real

than anything right now. This is the world we want to take to bed with us tonight.

But it's not bedtime yet. It's wonder time. Yes, it's late, but it's not too late. It's never too late for this . . .

I will grant peace in the land, and you will lie down
and no one will make you afraid.

LEVITICUS 26:6, NIV

Beach Butler Brigade

WE HAVE BEEN fortunate to visit some great beaches in the United States and even a few beyond our borders. But here is a beach resort we will not be visiting—ever: the Burj Al Arab in Dubai, United Arab Emirates.

We have nothing against an all-suite 321-meter-high hotel that is shaped like a giant ship's sail. And we think we could get used to being served by, as a host of advertisements puts it, "a brigade of highly trained butlers" during our vacation. (How many butlers are in a brigade, anyway?)

The problem is the price tag. One night in the least expensive suite in this beach resort will set you back more than $2,000, while the fanciest one will cost you north of $10,000. And that price does not include the "optional chauffeur-driven Rolls-Royce." Oh, *okay*.

Here's the thing: As we researched this and other high-end beach resorts, we found that many of them had *no* vacancies on several dates. Even those $10,000 rooms were booked for large chunks of time.

That amount isn't even write-a-bestseller money—it's win-the-lottery money.

And did you know that in the United States, the number of people buying lottery tickets exceeds the number who vote? Americans, perhaps more than any other country's citizens, want to be rich. Beach-resort rich. Or at least they think they do.

The truth is that people who are miserable when they're destitute tend to be miserable when they are rich—sometimes even *more* miserable. Those few "lucky" lottery winners quickly discover, for example, that their newfound fortune has brought with it family quarrels, tension in friendships, and a whole host of people and organizations with their hands out. You may have read stories about lottery winners, for example, whose spouses divorced them as soon as the check arrived, then demanded half of it.

Further, you've probably read about the train wrecks that some young celebrities are making of their lives. In a nationwide poll, the number one reason Americans gave for these celebrities' troubles was "too much money"—the answer cited by almost 80 percent of respondents.

No doubt they are onto something. In a collegiate study of life satisfaction, researchers analyzed twenty factors that might contribute to a person's happiness (relationships, career choices, health, and so on). The study concluded that nineteen of those factors did, in fact, matter. The one that didn't? A person's financial status.

Want even more evidence? Consider J. Paul Getty, the industrialist who founded Getty Oil Company. At the time of his death, his assets were valued at more than $2 billion. But considering he had been married and divorced five times, is such a lofty amount really so tantalizing? "A lasting relationship with a woman is only possible if you are a business failure," he said. At one point he even confessed to his friends, "I would give all my wealth for one successful marriage."

There's a revelation worth at least $2 billion. And throw in a brigade of highly trained beach butlers, too.

Those who love money will never have enough.
How meaningless to think that wealth
brings true happiness!

ECCLESIASTES 5:10

Uses for Sand

YOU LOVE THE way it looks. You love to play in it, even though you're not a kid anymore. You love the way it feels between your toes. Sand has many uses and benefits—including the way it naturally exfoliates your feet. (Everyone knows an exfoliated foot is a happy foot.)

There are, however, instances in which sand is not the best choice. It's no substitute for the special potting soil your wife asked you to pick up at the home-improvement store. It is not a delicious addition to your pancake batter (something we learned as children). And sand makes a lousy foundation.

You know the story—a wise man built his house on solid rock. And when storms came, the house stood strong. A foolish man built his house on sand with no firm foundation. When storms came, the house folded like a beach chair.

Hearing God's Word and *putting it into practice* is equivalent to building on a rock-solid foundation. And hearing

God's Word and *failing* to put it into practice? Well, that is building your house on a faltering foundation of sand.

Without the firm foundation of God's Word in our daily lives, we'd better have our insurance agents on speed dial. Because without it, we are building on the unstable, shifting, and untrustworthy surface of our own understanding.

Or even worse, we're building on the shifting sands of what's popular. What's trending. That's following Jesus on social media but not truly *following* Jesus. That's like putting sand in your gas tank.

A life not anchored to something solid is bound to fall apart when things get rough.

So while you're frolicking on the beach and enjoying the benefits of sand (can you feel the exfoliation?), remember that it's not a solid choice when it comes to foundations. Save the sand for playing, relaxation, and, perhaps, sanding.

If we want our house to withstand the storms of life, we need to avoid the sandy foundations of this world and build on the Rock.

[Jesus said,] "Everyone who hears these words of mine and puts them into practice is like a wise man who built his house on the rock. The rain came down, the streams rose, and the winds blew and beat against that house; yet it did not fall, because it had its foundation on the rock. But everyone who hears these words of mine and does not put them into practice is like a foolish man who built his house on sand. The rain came down, the streams rose, and the winds blew and beat against that house, and it fell with a great crash."

MATTHEW 7:24-27, NIV

Beach Church

A TEENAGE GIRL—adopted at birth—visited her biological mother one summer and (reluctantly) accompanied her to church in a small beach community. As the pastor began his sermon, the girl thought, *This guy is the worst preacher I've ever heard. He isn't funny or insightful like my pastor back home. He acts uncomfortable up there. And look at him—he's so tanned! Too bad he didn't spend as much time practicing his sermon as he likely did at the beach . . .*

The girl sat bored for the next twenty minutes, wishing her mother had let her sleep in, the way her parents back home did.

"And in conclusion . . ."

The girl sighed with relief. *Thank goodness that's over*, she thought. Then came a faint sniffling sound. Turning, she found a woman sitting next to her who was sobbing quietly and dabbing her eyes with a tattered tissue.

"That was just what I needed to hear," the woman

said. The girl's mom nodded sympathetically and gave the woman a fresh tissue from her purse.

Feeling a bit guilty, the girl swallowed hard. But she learned a valuable lesson that day: Through God's grace and provision, a message that might lack in style can still speak to the hearts of listeners.

Have you ever been afraid to write a poem, draw a picture, give a speech, or sing a song because you thought your talents weren't worthy of anyone's attention? If so, take heart. God doesn't expect you to be polished and perfect in your endeavors. He just expects you to be sincere and faithful. If you simply do your best, you can touch hearts.

Let love and faithfulness never leave you.

PROVERBS 3:3, NIV

The Throwaway Ritual

WHAT DO YOU do with the inevitable disappointments and hurts that life hands you? Many people internalize them and let them creep into their hearts—where they fester and create worry, pain, and despair. We like to hurl them into the deep.

If you go to the beach with us, you have to partake in The Ritual: You walk the sand. You grab whatever will make a suitable projectile—shells, stones, clumps of sand . . . anything but garbage, for the sea stomachs enough of that already.

As we throw every representative shell and stone, we pray: "God, please take this burden from me. I know You care about what it's doing to me. I commit it into Your hands. Please set me free from the pain and disappointment and frustration that it's causing me."

Yes, The Ritual is only symbolic. But it signifies something real.

Our kids sometimes protest: "I don't see why we are

doing this. You can't really throw away your problems." But a short while later, one of them will grab a chunk of sea glass and heave it. A few seconds of flight . . . a soft plunk . . . then a nod of satisfaction—or relief.

Can you truly throw away your problems in the sea? Depends on whom you are throwing them to.

Give your burdens to the LORD,
and he will take care of you.

Fire Coral

FLORIDA AND THE Caribbean are two of our favorite places to swim and snorkel. You can dive for conch shells and swim (very briefly) with stingrays in their liquid flight. But you need to be careful where you put your hands: Do *not* touch the fire coral.

Fire coral is a misnomer since it's not a coral at all. Rather it's an impostor from the related Hydrozoa class—an evil cousin of the jellyfish and sea anemone. Grab a fire coral "branch," and your hand will feel like you dipped it in a pot of boiling needles. As for the rash, the blisters, and the inflammation? You can google the pictures and see for yourself, if you wish. And if the stingers are not enough, rest assured that fire coral is also equipped with a sharp, calcified skeleton that will slice whatever the stingers missed.

Yes, a week at the beach can be hard on the hands. But every time we start to complain about a jellyfish sting or a stony-coral cut, we think of Jesus.

Hands that formed towering mountain ranges and

carved vast oceans should not have been bound like those of a common criminal or savagely pierced by spikes—but that's what happened. Merely living a normal life on earth would have been a supreme sacrifice for Jesus. He gave up heaven to become a lowly, born-in-a-barn human, just to be with the likes of us. To share in our pain, fatigue, hunger, anger, and persecution.

That's like you or me becoming a mollusk—with a tiny mollusk-size "brain" and ocean-sized problems. Imagine a life in which a good day consists of avoiding being chomped by a walrus.

But Jesus went beyond empathy . . . beyond merely walking in human sandals. He did more than live the life we know: He gave up His own.

He *allowed* His hands to be tied, to be punctured by nails.

He could have changed His mind at any point. He could have transported Himself back to the comforts of heaven, declaring, "I do not deserve this!" Or He could have fought off His persecutors. Hands that created a universe and restored crippled limbs and brought the dead back to life could have easily subdued a mob of thugs and hypocrites.

But Jesus did not raise hands in His own defense. It was us He was defending—from the curse of sin and death.

Today, those once-abused hands are held out to all humanity, longing to save anyone willing to accept their rescue. Despite all they have endured, those holy hands, once they lay hold of you, will never let you go.

Gathering the children up in his arms,
[Jesus] laid his hands of blessing on them.

MARK 10:16, MSG

Dr. Robot Will See You Now . . .

THE KNIFE IS coming for us.

Too many years of beach volleyball. Too many plunges off the paddleboard. Too many triathlons—when we weren't exactly in triathlon shape (or even "athlon" shape, for that matter).

Among the Hafer brothers, there are shoulders that need to be mended. Knees hoping to be scraped of mangled cartilage. Feet begging for fortification.

It's time to see our friendly neighborhood doctor . . . or perhaps our friendly neighborhood robot.

Robotic surgery is a trending innovation in the medical world. Robots are fixing damaged hearts, transplanting kidneys, and even removing cancer from people's bodies. Helping two aging athletes should be a day at the beach for R2-MD2, or whatever his name is.

Of course, the robots are not doing all this slicing and stitching on their own. Human doctors are still in charge, using computers to remotely control medical tools attached

to the robot's arms. Kind of like a gamer using a controller or computer keys to master a video game.

You know where we are going with this, right? Just as a doctor chooses to use a robot to get some of his work done, God has chosen people like us to be His hands here on earth.

What an honor, and what a responsibility—to feed the hungry, share the Good News, comfort the hurting, encourage the downtrodden, and protect the persecuted. May we all be up to the tasks at hand.

Never walk away from someone who deserves help;
your hand is God's hand for that person.

PROVERBS 3:27, MSG

Walking Wounded

LIFE—THE WORK AND worry and whim of it all! Muscles falter under its load. Eyes close from sheer exhaustion, but sleep proves elusive. One sound can eject you from slumber. Or even worse—you awaken for no reason at all. You lie mired in discomfort of body and mind that is impossible to describe.

The beach can be a source of renewal or resurrection, of course. But to be renewed is to have been old and worn. To be resurrected is to have been dead. Not every time do you hit the beach like a conquering hero, after all. Sometimes you step through the sand like a wounded soldier on the battlefield. The walk in the sunshine leaves you weak instead of invigorated.

What's the point of even going to the beach this summer? you wonder. *Why spend the time . . . why spend the money?*

But go you do, if only to avoid disappointing the family.

Then you stand on the shore and look up, look out, look around. And it's as if you have never seen before. This new,

138

old world . . . it's been there for ages. How have you failed to experience it like *this*—until right now?

Perhaps all life-giving discoveries are like this. Perhaps we must see the new thing in our old friend Nature in order to value the new possibilities in ourselves. When we contemplate a God-love as deep as the ocean, as vast as the sky, we can shake off the weariness and say, "I will rise again. I will love and not be limited."

Create in me a pure heart, O God,
and renew a steadfast spirit within me.

PSALM 51:10, NIV

Plumb Full?

WHENEVER WE GET a chance to take a group of kids or teens to the beach, we share one of our favorite object lessons . . .

First, we set a one-gallon glass jar in the sand or on a beach log or picnic table. Then we empty a bag of about a dozen fist-size rocks into the jar.

"Is this jar full?" we ask.

Because the rocks reach the top of the jar, the answer is usually yes.

Next comes the gravel, which we dump in so it settles among the rocks.

We ask again: "Is the jar full?"

By now they are onto us. "It's not plumb full," someone responded once. "It's only prit-near plumb full!" (Some of our youth group kids grew up in the country.)

Then we grab the sand by handfuls from the beach. We sprinkle it into the jar and shake gently. The sand sifts its way among the rocks and gravel.

"Full yet?"

"No!" the kids shout.

Our last ingredient is water from the lake or ocean. We pour it in until it's running over the brim.

At this point, we can convince the kids that the jar is finally full—though someone will usually note that we could still add Kool-Aid.

Now for the most important question: "What is the point of this fun demonstration?"

Recently a polite honor student raised her hand. "No matter how full your schedule is, you can always fit a few more things into it," she offered. Spoken like a true over-achiever. (Please pray for her.)

"No, no, no," corrected the girl's friend, shaking her head. "You're missing it. Imagine how things would have gone if the Hafer brothers had put the water, sand, and gravel in *before* the big rocks. How would that have worked out? If you don't put the big rocks in first, you'll never be able to squeeze them in later."

Her friend had it right. Think about the state of your personal and professional life. Is it full like the jar? You'll always be faced with setting priorities. And to be successful, you have to figure out what the "big rocks" are in your life. Things like relationships, rest, volunteer work, spirituality, or that personal quest you're passionate about.

Make sure you put those in the jar first, or the smaller stuff will crowd them out. Don't let your life tell merely a good story when, with a little planning on your part, it can tell a great one—a *full* one.

Seek first his kingdom and his righteousness,
and all these things will be given to you as well.

MATTHEW 6:33, NIV

A Sail with Attitude

WHEN WE HAFER brothers are hanging out on our luxury sailing yacht, we often think to ourselves, *How did we wind up in this crazy dream where we own a yacht—and why is that giant talking dolphin on our boat, wearing a neon tuxedo?*

So maybe it's only in our wildest dreams that we own a yacht—maybe only in our wildest dreams that we are even *near* a yacht. That's okay with us. The word *yacht* has too many consonants anyway.

Still, we love to *watch* boats with sails (of all sizes). What a miraculous thing to harness the power of the wind to go where you wish! But first, there's an important concept you must grasp: *attitude.*

One nautical glossary defines it as "position by bearings; orientation of a craft relative to its direction of motion." (By the way, to compliment an expert sailor, tell him or her, "Whoa, your glossary is totally nautical!")

Now if you're a sailor (especially an attitude sailor), you understand immediately what this definition means.

We are sailing challenged, so we humbly asked a smart guy who is sailing savvy. His answer? "Your position and the way you're pointing, especially when it comes to the wind, have everything to do with propelling you where you want to go."

We couldn't have said it better—even if we knew what we were talking about. In life, our position and the way we are pointed—our attitude toward God—determine our direction.

God made us free. He granted us the ability to choose our attitude toward Him and the rest of His creation. And the attitudes we choose will have a lot to do with thrusting us in good or bad directions.

Let's consider some of the good attitudes:

- Thankfulness
- Humility
- Worshipfulness
- Generosity

And just to make sure we don't run aground, here are some attitudes to avoid:

- Bitterness
- Arrogance
- Jealousy
- Selfishness
- Unforgiveness

Good news: You don't have to be an expert sailor or own a nautical glossary to know what a good attitude looks like. Better news: If you've fallen into one of the negative patterns, you can shift your sails and change it right now. Just take a look at your heart and ask, "What's my attitude?"

We hope it's totally nautical.

The purposes of a person's heart are deep waters,
but one who has insight draws them out.

PROVERBS 20:5, NIV

A Lonely Funeral

A PASTOR MADE frequent visits to a sickly woman in the days before her death. During their tortoise-slow walks together on the bay shore near her home, the woman complained constantly about her family and various former friends and business associates who had offended or betrayed her. The pastor noticed that she never said hello or even made eye contact with anyone who crossed their path as they ambled along the sandy shore.

The minister tried to admonish the woman against harboring a spirit of bitterness, especially because her days on earth were numbered. But he doubted he was getting through to her.

A few days after one of their sessions together, the minister got word that the woman had passed away. Just before her death, she had requested that the minister officiate her funeral. It would turn out to be one of the most memorable services of his long career.

As he took his place at the front of the church, the pastor

looked out at an empty sanctuary, save for the woman in her coffin. Now fighting back tears, he truly understood the depths of this woman's bitterness and the shroud of loneliness it had dragged over her life.

If you need incentive to maintain current relationships, rekindle an old friendship, or patch up an intrafamily rift, this should be it. Close relationships—even more than one's worldview or level of personal satisfaction—are the most meaningful ingredients in overall happiness.

Research sheds even more light on this truth: The book *Mental Health in Black America* studied core factors leading to a happy life. They are . . .

- Number of friends
- Closeness of these friends
- Closeness of family
- Relationships with coworkers and neighbors

Together, these four factors made up 70 percent of a person's overall happiness.

We wish that the story above were just an illustration. It's not. We come from a family of pastors, and we know that some funerals are lonely. We recall one service with only half a dozen attendees, including the deceased.

The lesson here? Sobering and simple: Don't die alone—by choosing to live alone.

Keep yourselves safe in God's love.

JUDE 1:21

Beach, Interrupted

WE WON'T MENTION them by name, but it's a sad fact that some beaches are truly annoying. You can't read a page of your novel or grab a minute of sun without being approached by a vendor hawking "revolutionary" sunscreen or some manner of deep-fried dough that has been rolled in sugar.

We call it "Beach, Interrupted."

Isn't it surprising that such minor irritations can swing a wrecking ball into your long-awaited beach escape? You could liken it to the way a tension headache robs you of sleep. The annoyance of telemarketers interrupting your dinnertime. Or say a corporate restructuring that puts the brakes on your career progress.

So, then, is it too much to ask for a few moments free of boisterous beach vendors?

When we get a case of "Beach, Interrupted" or "Life, Interrupted," we must step back and try to regain our perspective. Will the world stop turning if we don't quite make

that project deadline? Will babies no longer smile and orioles no longer sing if we can't do absolutely everything we want while on summer vacation? Will our jobs cease to be meaningful if a less deserving person is named "Associate of the Month"?

When we observe life through a clear lens, what is a traffic ticket or a flat tire compared to the vast scope of blessings already heaped upon us? And if we remember that those loud and out-of-control kids on the beach are loved wholly and eternally by almighty God, who cares if they keep us from that snooze we were hoping to catch?

What's more, what can possibly compare to the gift Jesus gave us when He took away our sins? Even when circumstances are hard and the beach is a bust, life is still good.

Because our God is *good*.

The Lord will indeed give what is good.

PSALM 85:12, NIV

The Blond Boy on the Beach

RUNNING ON THE beach one day up in northern Michigan, we tried to exchange a quick hello with Aaron, a blond boy sitting along our path.

It didn't work.

Aaron couldn't utter a single word: He was almost totally deaf. He was also legally blind, and his heart struggled to pump blood.

When Aaron was born with a rare genetic condition, doctors told his parents he would probably die before his first birthday. If by some miracle he lived to wheeze out that single candle, he would endure a life of little quality. He wouldn't be able to feed himself, walk, or communicate with anyone.

Aaron's parents listened to what the doctors said. But they listened to Jesus even more. They chose to see their son through Jesus' eyes.

Aaron's father, Steve, said they realized early on that Aaron was on a mission from God to change lives.

Aaron grew up to be a handsome, tan, blond-haired kid who learned how to get around in a wheelchair, feed himself, and communicate using hand signals. He laughed and smiled when something brought him joy, which happened frequently in Aaron's world.

Most important, his parents, sister, and friends discovered that if they moved closer, Aaron could recognize them. Such a feat had been impossible when he looked at them from a sterile distance.

If you got right up in Aaron's grill, he had just enough sense of sight, sound, and smell to know you were there. He'd greet you with a smile, a hug, a pat on the head.

Because of his limitations, Aaron focused intently on each person he interacted with. Those closest to him noted that he could discern how a person was feeling. He could sense things that others could not.

When he was sixteen, Aaron attended a summer church camp with his family. At one worship service, he tooled around the auditorium in his chair while dozens of people filled the room. Aaron sidled up to a sixty-something woman named Susie and reached out to her, brushing her

face with his hand and cooing a greeting. Susie leaned toward him, and he gave her a hug and a kiss on the cheek. Tears trickled down her face.

Several days before the camp began, Susie's husband had died, and she had been tempted to stay home. After all, this was a family camp, and now she would be alone.

Susie decided to give it a try, but seeing all the frolicking families was hard on her. Somehow, Aaron sensed Susie's pain. Of all the people at a crowded meeting, a legally blind teen spotted the one who needed him. Aaron and the widow became fast friends.

"If you want to greet Aaron or spend some time with him," his pastor, Dwight Nelson, said, "you begin by simply touching his shoulder. . . .

"You must draw close to him, for his ability to see and hear is very limited. You need to get closer to him than is normally a comfortable distance. When you make yourself known in that way, he may well smile, he may well want to touch you, take hold of your hair, and give you a hug, shake hands. And as you enter his life in that way, you feel blessed by him.

"This is what Aaron teaches us about knowing God and letting God be our teacher. . . . It does not work to shout a greeting to God as we rush by him in a hurry to be busy. If you want to know God, to be taught by him, to follow Christ, you must touch him."

The boy on the beach taught us that you cannot have a relationship with God when you are always distant from Him.

And he taught us without saying a word. We're glad we took the time to get close.

When you draw close to God, God will draw close to you.
JAMES 4:8, TLB

Postscript: Aaron Barg passed away at age eighteen. Around six hundred people from his community attended his visitation. Some waited in line for more than two hours to pay their respects.

Radio Love

WHAT IS LOVE, anyway?

On the sound systems at our favorite beach, the word pops up like dandelions.

Unfortunately, this love doesn't sound like the real deal.

Is love selfish or obsessive? Is it truly as shallow as a tide pool?

Is love a whim, usually driven by physical attraction? "I love you, baby!" in a pop song is better translated, "I am hot for you at this present moment—until someone more attractive comes into the picture."

God, the author of love, didn't design it to be a mere feeling. Yes, love involves emotions. But it is also a decision, an act of the will. Sometimes love is a struggle, something that requires constant effort. True love is caring about others—your spouse, kids, parents, and (gulp) parents-in-law—even if your love isn't reciprocated or appreciated. Love is a commitment that doesn't fade, regardless of consequences.

Real love is what Jesus displayed when He chose to

sacrifice Himself for the sake of all of us in this world. And He made this choice *knowing* that many would spurn or belittle His supreme sacrifice. Further, He knew that no one deserved this great gift of love. He knows the selfishness of the human heart. He knows every awful thing about every single person who has ever lived—and who ever will live. Yet He still gave Himself up.

The Lord of all creation, who knew you before you were born, has decided to love you. In spite of your mistakes. In spite of the indifference you might feel toward Him sometimes.

God, in His love, is committed to you. As you seek to follow Him, He will faithfully forgive, unconditionally accept, and perfectly love you always. He makes the effort, every day. And He wants us to try to do the same.

Wish we heard more of that at our beach.

Anyone who does not love does not know God,
for God is love.

1 John 4:8

A San Diego Savior

IF YOU HAPPEN to experience the misfortune of dealing with a flat tire or any other sort of vehicular malfunction on your way to the beach in San Diego, pray Thomas Weller finds you. He was destined to help from an early age.

Years ago on a lonely Illinois road, sixteen-year-old Thomas struggled to drive home in a blizzard. But the slick roads and strong winds were too much for him. He lost control of his car and smashed into a snowbank.

Shaken but unhurt, Thomas sat in his stuck car and waited. And waited. It seemed he'd been the only person to venture out on such a stormy night. For the longest time, not another car or truck was in sight.

Finally he got his miraculous break when a man stopped and helped Thomas free his car from the snowbank. Before long, the grateful teenager was home, safe and warm. Later that night, his thoughts churned up a powerful realization: *There wasn't any other traffic out there tonight. That man probably saved me from freezing to death!*

Not only did that act of mercy save Thomas's life—it also changed it. He's been on a mission of mercy ever since he was pulled out of that Illinois snowbank. Today, more than five decades later, he is known as the "San Diego Highwayman." An auto mechanic by trade, Thomas drives around in a classic old car on the lookout for drivers who are stranded.

Thomas has saved more than six thousand drivers, filling up empty gas tanks, changing flat tires, and pouring coolant into hissing radiators. He's rescued scared and lonely teenagers, church youth groups stuck in their vans, and busloads of soccer and beach-volleyball players.

Thomas accepts no pay for his services. He only asks that the people who've benefited from his mercy pass it along the next time they meet someone in trouble.

Long ago, Jesus preached a sermon to a crowd on a mountainside. "God blesses those who are merciful, for they will be shown mercy," He said (Matthew 5:7). Thomas Weller is a living example of Jesus' words.

There are those who cry tears of gratefulness for the assistance Thomas provides. Some even try to pay him. But

Thomas is motivated by love that flows from a thankful heart, not money. He just wants to share one of the most beautiful gifts of all: mercy. It's something that anyone can give—you don't have to be a grown-up or have lots of money. And when you consider its unique tendency to multiply and spread to others, you can see why mercy is the gift that keeps on giving.

Happy are the kind and merciful,
for they shall be shown mercy.
MATTHEW 5:7, TLB

Cleaning Up

WE WALK THE sands of Grand Traverse Bay on Lake Michigan . . . heads down, scanning the sunbaked sand. Not for a stone, shell, or shard of sea glass to pluck and pocket. Not for some treasure polished and delivered by the lake's waters.

Our prey are crushed Coors cans, burger-joint bags, and mateless shoes.

Why make the effort? It's a losing battle. *USA Today* reports that one in ten American beaches is not fit for swimming. Go online and view the evidence, if you dare. Like hunger, poverty, illiteracy, and crime, pollution can be expressed in figures. But none of these menaces are really statistics or even "problems." No, all are tragedies.

We can quantify the litter on the sand and the toxins lurking in the water, but sadly enough, numbers don't pierce apathy. What should kick our hearts barely even nudges our brains. Knowing is not the same as feeling.

Still we walk with bags in hand. Yes, we "know" the statistics. But we also feel. We care deeply about bringing joy

to those who share the planet with us. And the fate of this beach can affect the fate of all beaches.

As children of God, our mandate is to care for His creation. So we deal with the beach debris before us, hoping others across the world are doing likewise. Large corporations are not going to do this work any more than they will raise your child or tend your garden. With some tasks, smaller is better.

Will today's cleanup make a difference? We answer this question with another: Is there hope in seeing the good that needs to be done . . . and doing it?

The earth and every good thing in it belongs
to the Lord and is yours to enjoy.

1 CORINTHIANS 10:26, TLB

All That Sand Stuff

A portable, waterproof Bluetooth speaker.

A sand castle kit for the kids.

A sand anchor for the portable umbrella.

A sandless beach mat. (No kidding.)

An inflatable foot rest.

A foldable teakwood rinse-off platform.

A small gang of beach chairs.

Yes, the family near us on the beach had it all, right down to the deluxe beach cart they used to transport most of the above items. (Why not bring the joy of lugging a suitcase through the airport . . . to the beach?)

We confess to a few envy pangs over some of the stuff. The sandless beach mat made it onto our wish list, if only to see whether it actually worked.

What's on your life's Wish List? What do you pine for but don't possess?

For many, money and material possessions top their

lists. Americans have a possession obsession: We want faster computers and bigger, better TVs—but smaller music-delivery systems. Just as long as "smaller" comes with longer battery life and more memory. And who wouldn't love a foldable teakwood rinse-off platform to remove all those annoying remnants of nature after a day seaside?

For others, status, image, and success are the ultimate prizes. Some want to be the next pop star, game show champion, or proud owner of a new face and better beach body.

Conversely, Jesus instructed His followers to take with them only the bare necessities when they set out on a journey. "Travel light," Jesus advised.

As the day unspooled, we watched our beach-neighbor family struggle to keep track of all their stuff.

"Where's the big bucket for the sand castle set?"

"Don't splash water on the [waterproof] speaker! It was very expensive!"

"Where are my brand-new Bentley sunglasses?" (Uh, they are atop your head.)

The family seemed stressed as they shook the sand off

their sandless beach mat and loaded up their cart. They left before the long evening fell and the rumpled surface of the water transformed from blue to silver.

About an hour later, we tossed a few damp and sandy towels into our own deluxe beach totes (also known as our reusable canvas grocery bags). Even after a long day at the beach, the bags were light to carry.

Don't love money; be satisfied with what you have.

HEBREWS 13:5

Beach Reads

JUST BEYOND THE documents of work and worry and a little past your overstuffed in-box, something is lurking . . . waiting . . . crouching. As soon as you settle into your beach chair, it pounces!

Ah, the beach book . . . you've waited so long for this . . .

What can we say about the world of beach reads? Here stand the books you don't *have* to read. The books you open with the spirit of an adventurer. The books that assure you, "We won't preach down to you. We portray life as it is, or as it could be. Inside you will find surprise, intrigue, insight, and the high spirit of life itself."

It doesn't matter whether the authors are famous or obscure or practitioners of fiction or nonfiction—as long as they tell the *truth*. As long as they bring wonder, humor, and love to their work.

Some books make you want to leap from your beach towel and start changing the world. Others help you bear burdens with more patience and faith. And a few simply allow you to escape yourself for a time . . . to journey into a world beyond your own.

But all great books glow with the fire of life. All of them let you know, "You have made a friend. You are less alone in this world than when you turned that first magic page. And thanks for taking me to the beach."

Truthful words stand the test of time.

PROVERBS 12:19

Abraham Lincoln's Mad Skills

IT MAY BE an odd question, but here goes: Of all the presidents since America's founding, which one would you pick to take along on your summer vacation?

In many of our polls, Abraham Lincoln tops the list.

But is that a good idea—especially if summer vacation means time at the beach? Could Honest Abe even swim?

You might be surprised. Lincoln was no fish out of water. As a child and a young adult, he swam in lakes near his Indiana home, then later in the Sangamon River when he moved to Illinois. One of Lincoln's fellow soldiers recalled that "very few men in the army could successfully compete with Mr. Lincoln, either in wrestling or swimming; he well understood both arts."

Lincoln had mad skills, in and out of the water. Here's a Lincolnesque skill we all should employ in the inevitable conflicts that occur on trips to the beach—and throughout the rest of life too . . .

Consider the matter of Edwin Stanton, secretary of war for the Union during the Civil War.

At one point during the war, Stanton became enraged at a Union general who he felt was defying authority. Stanton shared his anger with his boss, the president. Lincoln listened, then suggested Stanton write a sharp letter expressing how he felt.

Stanton took his advice at once. His pen was like a hypodermic needle, injecting every drop of his anger into scathing words scratched on paper. Then he showed the letter to Lincoln, brandishing it like a sword. The president read carefully.

"You don't want to send that letter," Lincoln said. "Put it in the stove. That's what I do when I have written a letter while I am angry. It's a good letter, and you've had a good time writing it and feel better. Now, burn it, and write another letter."

Indeed, one of Lincoln's hallmarks was his wisdom. And he was wise enough to know that angry people say things they don't mean. And even when they say something they

do mean, they say it in such a cruel way that the message gets lost in the madness.

That's why Lincoln made a practice of writing two letters to address difficult people and situations. The first ended up burning in a woodstove or being torn to bits and sprinkled like confetti into a waste bin.

Think about Lincoln the next time you're typing an angry e-mail. Then save a draft and come back to it later, when you're no longer boiling inside. Similarly, before you start shouting at someone—in person or through your phone—think about what you're going to say and how you should say it. Rehearse the conversation in your mind, considering how you would feel if *you* were on the receiving end.

This approach to handling anger is not just presidential; it's biblical. The Bible doesn't command, "Never, ever get mad." It says, "In your anger do not sin" (Ephesians 4:26, NIV). Everyone gets angry. Even a president. The key to effective, harmonious relationships is *how* we handle anger. If you have to blow off some steam, go ahead and do it. Just make sure no one gets burned in the process.

Remember that what you say and do in anger cannot be unsaid or undone. To put it another way . . . which would you rather have in the trash bin—that fuming e-mail, or one of your relationships?

Don't let the sun go down while you are still angry.

EPHESIANS 4:26

One Jet Ski, Gently Used

WHEN WE WERE in college, our friend Steve bragged, "I'm not going to even consider a job unless it pays eighty thousand a year!"

Steve got caught up in the competition of pursing a lucrative career. He truly wanted to open his own sporting goods store, but some of his friends laughed at that goal.

So Steve went into another field. He made stupid money working insane hours. He's also been laid off twice—because he's in a cutthroat business.

"Money can't buy happiness" is as true as the sun in the sky for him (never mind that he dislikes old adages). Steve can afford a lot of expensive toys, but as he says, "The problem with toys is that you outgrow them so quickly."

Steve is trying to sell his Jet Ski, which he used at the lake near his home—once. His online ad reads, "For Sale: one Jet Ski, very gently used."

Our friend has learned that if your career isn't linked

to your life's passion, you are going to feel empty and unfulfilled.

When he heard we were writing a book, Steve said, "Tell your readers, 'Don't follow the money. Enough money will find you when you do what you love. God will provide. Follow your passion. Oh, and if anyone wants to buy a Jet Ski . . .'"

Give me neither poverty nor riches,
but give me only my daily bread.

PROVERBS 30:8, NIV

The Beach as Happy Place

ASK OUR YOUNGER kids why they love the beach so much, and you're likely to get an answer like "Because the beach is my happy place!"

Don't we all yearn to find our happy place?

Happiness was important enough for the Founding Fathers to claim as an "unalienable right" in the Declaration of Independence. But of all the rights we citizens expect—or crave—it is perhaps the most elusive and the hardest to define. You know whether you're old enough to vote—or not. You know you cannot be forced to quarter a soldier in your home. But do you know if you're happy?

Maybe that question is so perplexing because the pursuit of happiness can defy logic. Research reveals that high-dollar, prestigious jobs like doctor and lawyer often don't make the top ten when it comes to the most rewarding occupations.

Meanwhile, low-paying, often thankless vocations like pastor and volunteer coordinator ranked second and third,

respectively, in a recent *Forbes* survey. (The rest of the top five: nursing home director, first; clinical supervisor, fourth; and hospice nurse, fifth.)

The three jobs rated least meaningful were assistant fast-food manager, account director, and fast-food cook.

On a similar note, the average American's buying power has tripled since 1956. And just think of the medical and technological advances that have emerged in the past half century. Yet the number of people who say they are happy has remained virtually unchanged—around 30 percent.

Life is often a pursuit of this elusive thing called happiness—a search that is more fruitful once we learn that true happiness isn't about fame, fortune, or professional success. It might be as close as the next song on your playlist, the dog slumbering at your feet, or the old friend who's waiting for your phone call.

We have learned that we are more likely to find our happy place when . . .

- we lift our eyes from the touch screen now and then to see how blue the sky is;

- we put away the smartphone and spend some time with paintbrush or pen, garden or guitar;
- we seek the blessing of silence amid the rush and noise of life; and
- we remember the advice we give our kids when they clamber up a sand dune on the beach: It's all about how happily you climb—not how high.

Oh, the joys of those who trust the LORD.

PSALM 40:4

Beach Volleyball

WHEN WE PLAY beach volleyball, we love to serve. Sometimes too much. We've heard ourselves saying things like "I demand to serve!" and "I can serve better than anyone here!" (Friends on our various sand volleyball teams would beg to differ with the latter.)

The irony of mixing boasting and serving is not lost on us. In the largest and best sense of the word, serving should be about humility, especially in our relationships.

Human relationships, even the best of them, are never perfect. Thus, our interactions with family and friends are sources of great joy—but also extreme frustration and even deep pain.

Have you noticed that when people show love by putting others' needs ahead of their own, rough waters are usually calmed?

Unfortunately, however, the real-life version of relationships is often selfish. Think about how many times you've been asked, "What do you look for in a friend?" "What's your

idea of the perfect mate?" But have you *ever* been asked, "What do you hope you can bring to your friendships?" or "What kind of employee do you aspire to be?"

Did those last two questions seem odd? Thank the twenty-first century's mantra: *All Me, All the Time.* Have you *ever* heard of anyone ending a job or a friendship with the (honest) words "I don't think *I* was bringing enough to the table"? Probably not.

Is it any wonder, then, that we tend to view all kinds of connections through suspicious eyes?

We shouldn't have to live in this bizarre economy in which we try to gain as much as we want from others while giving as little as we can.

Friendships, businesses, and families built on that paradigm will go bankrupt. Relationships need a better model: If we, with open hearts, choose to serve one another, putting our own agendas last, we will reap big, hefty bushels of love and joy.

Does this sound like a paradox? Well, consider how often Jesus taught that life proves paradoxical: A small mustard seed becomes a huge tree. Those willing to fall in at the end of the line end up getting jumped to the front. Give stuff away like there's no tomorrow, and you'll get it back with interest. Clutch on to stuff with a kung fu grip, and it'll wither and die.

What does this have to do with your business associates, friends, or significant other? Simple—if you are keeping score with any of these folks, you are playing the wrong game.

Let's discard the scorecards. Instead, we need to start asking ourselves questions like *What can I bring to the table in my relationships?* and *What needs do those around me have— and how can I help meet them?*

We promise that this approach, the one Jesus modeled so well, will free you to be the kind of friend, mate, parent, coworker, whatever . . . that people will thank God for.

Wouldn't you like to play the relationship game this way? If so, it's your turn to serve.

The humble will see their God at work and be glad.

PSALM 69:32

Comfort Zone Beach

AND NOW, DEAR friends, we leave you with this prayer—a fitting end to our time at the beach. May all your days—beachy or not—be filled with the warmth and light of Divine Love.

Dear God,
It's no secret . . . I love my little slice of my favorite beach!
When foreign umbrellas stake their claim on my sand,
I declare invasion by a hostile nation.

Yes, as do so many others, I relish my comfort zones . . .
Like the well-known routes around my city. Those primo
pit stops for a cappuccino.

The people who "get" me. The situations I can control.
The stuff I'm comfortable with. The rewards that are certain
and the risks that are tiny.

I confess that even when making the effort to reach
out to others, I don't reach very far. Familiar churches and
charities receive my donations—in amounts that don't strain
my budget. Volunteer work? I hit the same places as my

friends so someone else can do the unpleasant stuff—or deal with the people who make me uncomfortable. You know . . . the ones who don't look, act, talk, or even smell like me.

Please, God, remind me that my beach is not my beach. Show me where I need to quit making excuses and start making a difference. Maybe with a member of my family—someone who needs my encouragement. Or perhaps I could help with a need in my community.

Lord, I want sharp eyes that focus on the boundaries you're calling me to break . . . and the guts to step across, no matter how uncomfortable it may be. Lead me to new vistas—frontiers that cannot be accessed by a search engine.

And the next time I hit the beach? You can count on me. I'll sign a peace treaty with those alien umbrellas. Good-bye, war-torn MCZ (My Comfort Zone)—"wherever the Spirit of the Lord is, there is freedom" (2 Corinthians 3:17).

Thank you, Father. Amen.

Love from the center of who you are; don't fake it.

ROMANS 12:9, MSG

ACKNOWLEDGMENTS

We write every book as if it could be our last. It keeps us focused. It keeps us from pulling words like punches. But we hope this book is not the finale. We want to continue our long relationship with Chip MacGregor, our agent, who has kept believing in us when others have doubted.

We want another chance to win the attention and support of Becky Brandvik, whose vision and passion for this book have been a leap into the cool surf for two parched wordcombers.

And we want to sail from Book's Beginning to Book's End with Anisa Baker, the finest editor we have ever worked with. (She's especially good in choppy waters. Trust us.)

NOTES

GOD IS STUCK ON YOU, 16

We also recommend Peter Ekblom and Rupert Timpl's book
The Laminins, published in 1996 by Harwood Academic
Publishers.

COUNTING THE GRAINS OF SAND, 25

For more advice on time management, we recommend Lewis
Timberlake's book *First Thing Every Morning*, published in
2013 by Simple Truths LLC.

BAD BIRDS, 58

The authors thank Kimberly Miller for her brainstorm to
write about World War II carrier pigeons. For more on
the story of World War II, see Joe Razes's article "Pigeons
of War," *America in WWII*, accessed October 7, 2016,
http://www.americainwwii.com/articles/pigeons-of-war/.

COFFEE WITH JESUS?, 63

"Many of the 2.25 billion cups of coffee" Tori Avey, "The Caffeinated
History of Coffee," PBS: Food, April 8, 2013, http://www.pbs
.org/food/the-history-kitchen/history-coffee/.

"upwards of 400 million in the US" Kitchen Daily, "America's Coffee
    Obsession: Fun Facts That Prove We're Hooked," *Huffington
    Post*, November 2, 2011 (updated February 27, 2015),
    http://www.huffingtonpost.com/2011/09/29/americas
    -coffee-obsession_n_987885.html.

THREE STEPS ON THE BEACH, 70

"only about one in ten adults who have attempted it has completed the
    swim" William E. Schmidt, "Calais, Here I Come: Channel
    Swim Endures," *New York Times*, August 5, 1993, http://www
    .nytimes.com/1993/08/05/world/calais-here-i-come
    -channel-swim-endures.html.

"that man had worn a special wet suit" Scott Zornig in "What's
    Wrong with Marathon Swimming II?," The Daily News
    of Open Water Swimming, September 12, 2011,
    http://dailynews.openwaterswimming.com/2011/09
    /whats-wrong-with-marathon-swimming-ii.html.

"at 5:15 a.m." and "It's a shame if that gets in the way of what you
    call endeavor" "Tom Gregory—The youngest person ever
    to swim the English Channel," YouTube video, 14:30, from
    an interview with Thomas Gregory aired by BBC Radio 4

Saturday Live on April 16, 2016, posted by "BRST," April 19,
  2016, https://www.youtube.com/watch?v=2YQ0Iln97lY.

"WORMS ON THE BEACH" WITH CHARLES SPURGEON, 91

"What hundreds of little mounds" and *"That is all we [humans] do"*
  Charles Spurgeon, *The Essential Works of Charles Spurgeon:
  Selected Books, Sermons, and Other Writings,* ed. Daniel Partner
  (Uhrichsville, OH: Barbour, 2009), 780.
"I had always heard" and *"Sir, usually I do preach for souls"*
  Attributed to Charles Spurgeon
We are also grateful to our dear friend Dr. Eric Sparrman for his
  insights and stories about Charles Spurgeon.

GO, LEMMINGS!, 94

"You are who you roll with" This is one of the Hafer brothers'
  favorite TobyMac sayings. The last time Todd heard it, he
  and Toby were enjoying fish tacos in Nashville. Ah, fish
  tacos . . . like having the beach inside a tortilla!

THANKS FOR NOTHING, 98

"Gratitude is the key to happiness" Attributed to C. S. Lewis (and
  one of our favorite refrigerator magnets)

DRASTIC MEASURES, 101

"According to Wired magazine" "What Is Your Body Worth?"
DataGenetics, accessed June 2016, http://www.datagenetics
.com/blog/april12011/ and Scott Carney, "Inside the Business
of Selling Human Body Parts," *Wired*, January 31, 2011,
https://www.wired.com/2011/01/ff_redmarkets/.

MOOMAW!, 107

"If I didn't start painting" Bill Swainson, ed., *Encarta Book of
Quotations* (New York: St. Martin's Press, 2000), 389.
"Life is what we make it" "Grandma Moses Is Dead at 101;
Primitive Artist 'Just Wore Out,'" On This Day, *The Learning
Network* (blog), *New York Times*, December 14, 1961,
http://www.nytimes.com/learning/general/onthisday
/bday/0907.html.

ZIPPING UP THE DETAILS, 113

For more information about YKK, see Benjamin Fulford,
"Zipping Up the World," *Forbes*, November 24, 2003,
http://www.forbes.com/global/2003/1124/089.html and
"YKK," *Outside*, July 30, 2015, http://www.outsideonline
.com/2003196/ykk.

A PASSION FOR COMPASSION, 115

"While our soldiers can stand and fight . . . how to meet it" Attributed
    to Clara Barton

A FRIEND IN HIGH PLACES (REALLY, REALLY HIGH
PLACES), 118

"One particular star in our galaxy's Eta Carinae star system" We
    learned this fact from Max Lucado during one of his
    inspirational talks.

"If you could scoop just one spoonful" "r-p process movie," The
    JINA Center for the Evolution of the Elements, accessed
    September 14, 2016, http://www.jinaweb.org/movies/
    rp_movie.htm.

BEACH BUTLER BRIGADE, 122

*"the number of people buying lottery tickets exceeds the number who
    vote"* See George Jeng, "How many people in the US buy
    lottery tickets every year?" Quora, August 19, 2013,
    https://www.quora.com/How-many-people-in-the-US
    -buy-lottery-tickets-every-year and "2012 Voter Turnout
    Report," Bipartisan Policy Center, November 8, 2012,
    http://bipartisanpolicy.org/library/2012-voter-turnout/.

"In a nationwide poll" David Niven, *100 Simple Secrets of Happy People* (San Francisco: HarperCollins, 2006), n.p.

"A lasting relationship with a woman" Bevis Hillier, "The Great Getty: The Life and Loves of J. Paul Getty—Richest Man in the World by Robert Lenzner (Crown: $18.95; 304 pp.): The House of Getty by Russell Miller (Henry Holt: $17.65; 362 pp.)" (book reviews), *Los Angeles Times*, March 23, 1986, http://articles.latimes.com/1986-03-23/books/bk-5461 _1_j-paul-getty.

"I would give all my wealth" "Billionaire J. Paul Getty Is Dead at 83," *Chicago Tribune*, June 6, 1976, http://archives. chicagotribune.com/1976/06/06/page/1/article /billionaire-j-paul-getty-is-dead-at-83.

A SAIL WITH ATTITUDE, 143

"One nautical glossary" United States Coast Guard Auxiliary Interpreter Corps, "Glossary of Nautical Terms: English–Japanese," June 29, 2012, http://icdept.cgaux.org/pdf_files /English-Japanese-Nautical-Terms.pdf.

A LONELY FUNERAL, 146

"Research sheds even more light on this truth" Harold W. Neighbors
and James S. Jackson, eds., *Mental Health in Black America*
(Thousand Oaks, CA: SAGE Publications, 1996), n.p.

THE BLOND BOY ON THE BEACH, 151

"If you want to greet Aaron" Bob Smietana, "Confirming Aaron,"
The Covenant Companion, August 2005, http://www
.covchurch.org/resources/files/2010/05/0508-Confirming
-Aaron.pdf.

CLEANING UP, 160

"USA Today reports" Hoai-Tran Bui, "Yuck! 1 in 10 U.S. beaches
unsafe for swimming," *USA Today*, June 30, 2014, http://www
.usatoday.com/story/news/nation/2014/06/25/beaches
-polluted-pollution-water-runoff-sewage-bacteria/11349409/.

ABRAHAM LINCOLN'S MAD SKILLS, 167

"very few men in the army" In Douglas L. Wilson and Rodney O.
Davis, eds., *Herndon's Informants: Letters, Interviews, and
Statements about Abraham Lincoln* (Urbana and Chicago:
University of Illinois Press, 1998), 554.

"You don't want to send that letter" Paul F. Boller Jr., *Presidential Anecdotes* (New York, Oxford University Press, 1996), 135.

We are grateful to the staff of the Lincoln Home National Historic Site in Springfield, Illinois, for sharing many facts and stories about Abraham Lincoln, especially his early years. We also recommend the fine biography, *A. Lincoln: A Biography*, by Ronald C. White Jr. (New York: Random House, 2010).

THE BEACH AS HAPPY PLACE, 173

"the average American's buying power has tripled since 1956" and *"the number of people who say they are happy"* A. R. Bernard, *Happiness Is . . . : Simple Steps to a Life of Joy* (New York: Simon & Schuster, 2007), vi.